★ *Vincent Lopez says:*

"Numerology is a method of timing your decisions and actions with the rhythms of life"

With amazing accuracy

he predicted events such as riots in U.S. cities
and correctly analyzed personalities such as
Richard Nixon

Using insights only numerology can provide!

Now Mr. Lopez summarizes for the
layman this amazing science and shows
you how you can apply it to your own
life and problems. You simply add and
subtract the numbers that *belong to you*
and apply them to the explanations NU-
MEROLOGY provides.

*You'll learn about yourself and those
you love, what years will be crucial to
your happiness and how to make the most
of them. Let numerology guide you on
a vital journey to self-discovery and self-
fulfillment.*

Other Signet Books of Related Interest

123456789123456789123456789123456789123456

Numerology

123456789123456789123456789123456789123456

by VINCENT LOPEZ

A SIGNET BOOK

Published by
THE NEW AMERICAN LIBRARY

SIGNET TRADEMARK REG. U.S. PAT. OFF. AND FOREIGN COUNTRIES
REGISTERED TRADEMARK—MARCA REGISTRADA
HECHO EN CHICAGO, U.S.A.

SIGNET BOOKS are published by
The New American Library, Inc.,
1301 Avenue of the Americas, New York, New York 10019

FIRST PRINTING, MARCH, 1969

PRINTED IN THE UNITED STATES OF AMERICA

ACKNOWLEDGMENTS

The illustration of early European numbers on page 129 is from *The History of Mathematics* by David Eugene Smith (New York: Dover Publications, Inc., 1958) and is used with the permission of the publisher.

All other drawings of numbers and symbols were prepared especially for this volume by Susan Mayer.

CONTENTS

Foreword   9

Part One: FORECASTING AT A GLANCE   15
   Your Personal Year   21
   Your Personal Month and Day   37

Part Two: YOUR PATH OF DESTINY   47
   Your Destiny Number   49
   Your Life Cycles   55

Part Three: YOUR NAME   83
   How to Calculate the Number Value of Names   87
   Names and Numbers   96
   Missing Letter Numbers   105

Part Four: NUMBERS AND PHILOSOPHY   115
   Synthesis and Assemblations   117
   The Origin of Numbers   124
   Planets and Numbers   131
   The Zodiac   142
   Hidden Numbers   144

Remember this: Numerology is neither a religion nor a form of fortune-telling; rather it is a method of timing your decisions and actions with the universal rhythm of life.

VINCENT LOPEZ

FOREWORD

YOU MAY WONDER why someone like myself who has swung a baton to sweet music on a bandstand and has given out with the finger technique on the ivory keys all his life now suddenly should beat the keys of a typewriter in the hope of turning out a successful book on numerology.

"How come," you may ask, "does a musician offer a number system applied to human destiny when the subject seems so completely out of his line?"

But there's where you are wrong.

A strong affinity exists between music and mathematics. The correlation between numbers and the tones of the chromatic scale was established as a principle in the sixth century before Christ by the Greek philosopher Pythagoras. The happy marriage between numbers and the sound of music has always fascinated me, and, of course, I come by this enthusiasm naturally as a musician.

About twenty-five years ago, the Science of Numbers came to my attention. It immediately aroused my interest and I began to study it with experts. As years went by, I experimented with its merits in relation to my personal problems. Then I started my "Forecasting Time" from the Hotel Taft bandstand, helping hundreds of people to work out their bewildering problems. I also commented on numbers over the radio, on TV, and through my articles in the daily papers and in various magazines. One day someone suggested: "Why don't you write a book on numerology?" So you see, this task was thrust upon me by my friends. I now agree that they had a good idea.

But we all know there is a big jump from theory to practice. Numerology is good only if it can prove itself workable in our daily life and can help untangle the maze of emergencies as they arise during the course of a year. I can honestly state that an overwhelming percentage of forecasts I've made have come true. That applies not only to cases in which I have analyzed the numberscopes of individuals but also to predictions on current events which have found their way into print.

The *printed* word is what counts when you wish to check on a forecaster. Therefore I want to give you here quotations from articles and books, in which I have made prophecies that have been verified.

On May 31, 1940, I told a New York *World-Telegram* reporter that Mussolini would go into war on June 10th, 1940.

On August 27, 1939, in Danton Walker's column, I said that President Roosevelt would be re-elected and that Hitler would not die in the year 1940.

My prophecy of the break-up of Roumania and the end of King Carol's rule, with complete loss of power and territory in the fall of 1940 came true in September.

I said: "Italy stands to lose Ethiopia in 1941."

I wrote: "Stalin will continue to play along with Germany until 1941."

On March 21, 1941, I said: "Before 1944 this war will have merged into another war." This came to pass, of course, through the Japanese attack on Pearl Harbor, creating a second war in the Western hemisphere.

I wrote, again in Danton Walker's column, on March 21, 1941, that "Yugoslavia will be lined up with the Axis. Prince Paul will be deposed and a puppet government set up under someone else's rule, probably the eighteen-year-old King Peter. This should occur between March 21st and

April 1st." It took place March 27th. I added: "Greece will undergo decisive changes in her government regime and could lose an ally (not England, however), in April." This also happened, since she lost Yugoslavia.

In January, 1942, I wrote: "U.S.A.—The President may suffer a personal loss," which proved to be his mother.

Well, enough of the past. Let us turn to today.

The following are questions and answers from my book *What's Ahead*, written in 1943.

WHAT WILL HAPPEN TO THE UNITED STATES?

"America will emerge from this war, and in the peace to come, as the most powerful nation on earth, and as the leading people in the Western hemisphere."

DO WE FACE THE PROSPECT OF RACE RIOTS?

"Yes, there is considerable unhappy experience in store for the various minorities, since the racial issues will be dragged into the presidential campaign, increasing bitterness."

WILL LONDON REMAIN THE CAPITAL OF THE BRITISH EMPIRE?

"No! London will remain the capital of the British Isles, but the British Empire as we know it will not survive the present war."

WHAT WILL BECOME OF INDIA?

"India will be entirely on her own feet in the postwar organization of nations. She will first gain her freedom as a dominion, and then as a fully independent nation. She will gain her independence in 1947."

WHAT TYPE OF GOVERNMENT WILL FRANCE HAVE AFTER THE WAR?

"France will establish an entirely new form of democracy, and the nation will be restored in a big way. The old animosity between France and Germany will disappear completely."

Of Japan I said that it was a natural ally of the U.S.A. for which I was severely criticized. But the late Paul Clancy, publisher of *American Astrology* magazine, came to my defense in the March issue, 1942. He stated: "We should not forget that even though the horoscope of the Japanese Constitution may reveal a basis for amity, this does not deny a temporary liberty of action in the matter of quarreling with what was probably the best friend they had in the world. As Mr. Lopez expressed it: 'Japan at the present time is governed by a very war-like cabinet, which will stop at nothing. But by March, 1942, the people will begin to see and feel that they are being misdirected.' "

I predicted President Kennedy's assassination, and that Lyndon B. Johnson was a man of destiny.

On October 30, 1963, at the Art Director's Club in New York City, during a lecture I gave, I said that President Kennedy would have a tragic end. In Nick Kenny's column in the *New York Daily Mirror* I said on September 27, 1962, that Lyndon B. Johnson is a man of destiny, that in the next year he would emerge as one of the most sensational personalities of the Administration.

Also, in Nick Kenny's column in the *Daily Mirror,* I said on July 27, 1963, that "the stars are not right for 'Rocky'— he will not be nominated for the Presidency in 1964. I have always maintained that he would become Governor, but President of the U.S.A. never."

In my "Lopez Looks at the Numbers" column in Washington's *Roll Call,* October 17, 1968, issue, I made the following predictions:

Richard Nixon will be elected as our next President, but it will be a close election.

Spiro Agnew will be a great asset to Nixon . . . a good balance.

Wallace's intervention in this past campaign will result in the evolvement of a third party, probably by 1972.

Hy Gardner's column in the *Miami Herald* of December, 1967, carried my prediction that Jackie Kennedy would not marry Lord Harlech; that she would marry a much older man, most likely a foreigner who is famous in a field other than politics, before December, 1968.

Regarding Russian aggression: Russia will not stop with the Czechoslovak situation. Her next move will be into West Germany.

There will be more intensified flare-ups in the Middle and Near East which will go on for another thirty-two years.

Japan will become a world power second to the United States, its system based on our democratic society. It will eventually be the leader of the yellow race.

Our civilization is leaving the Piscean era, and we are entering the Aquarian age. The Aquarian age is ruled by water and the products of water. This will be a good time for investments in stocks, and organizations pertaining to the ocean and its products. There is more wealth in the ocean than there is on earth.

1976 will be one of the most crucial years in the history of our country.

Much has been said and written about Armageddon. It will occur in the Near East between now and the year 2000.

But there is another side to numerology, the help it can give individuals. Their problems are a matter of privacy, and in many cases of deepest secrecy. Therefore discretion forbids that I mention predictions I've made to prominent personages and celebrities of stage and screen who, as a matter of integrity, shall be nameless.

You too, reader, may have your cherished secrets you may want to ponder over privately. Therefore we give you a simple number method which will enable you to be your own "do-it-yourself" numerologist.

Yours in Cosmic Truth,

VINCENT LOPEZ

I

Forecasting at a Glance

NUMEROLOGY IS A LIFELONG study and its mastery is a full-time job. But who can give time to the science of numbers? Who has the leisure and interest to delve into the profundity of this fascinating philosophy? Most people are content with some highlight information that will indicate the direction they ought to follow in the pursuit of success and happiness.

Therefore we offer a short-cut technique of numerology which is accurate yet simple. This system can be likened to a road map from which the minor traffic centers—the small cities and villages—have been omitted. Only the major routes are indicated, and this information is sufficient for the ordinary motorist to get him to the place of his destination.

This method of numbers will instruct you in the nature of the vibrations that confront you, what your timing should be, and how to battle logically and psychologically with everyday problems. In this manner life will be easier for you to master and many difficulties with fellow-beings should be eliminated.

Two items of information are necessary as a basis for this simple numerology system:

1) The number vibration of the current year.
2) The number vibration of your month and day of birth.

Correlate these numbers and you will be able to determine the value of any given day, month or year. This is the vital guidepost we require for the timing of our important decisions and actions.

Of course, if grave problems or unusual complications arise in your destiny, you should consult a professional numerologist who can supply the minute details you may be unable to obtain from this short-cut technique.

HOW IT IS DONE

First calculate the vibrations of the current year. Let's take 1969 for our example.

The *19* can be called the *name* of the century. For the *19* will be tagged to this present century until the next one, which will carry the vibration of *20*. It will be ushered in by the year 2000. Until then every year will have the *19* in its number.

This *19* must be reduced to a single digit as follows:

1 plus *9* equals *10,* reduced to *1.*

The *1* vibration is the essence and soul of our present century. It is the number of the pioneer and the originator, and believe me, many innovations will occur, new concepts will loom upon mental and spiritual horizons, and these will be accepted generally by the public.

In fact, between today and year 2000 a new civilization will be born, a major war will be fought and new ideologies will have been established not only in these United States but all over the world.

So much for the number value of our present century: *1.*

Now comes the specific "year" vibration. In our case it is a *69* (of the year 1969). Add the *6* to the *1,* the result is *7.* Add this *6* of the current year to the *1* number of the century, and the total is *7. 1969 is a 7 year.*

This *7* of the year 1969 is a symbol, and it indicates that it is a good time for self-reflection. Find out what the *7* stands for in the chapter where the numbers from *1* to *9* are explained. You will discover that the *7* is a sabbatical year. It is not one of the best times to start new projects. It is a good time for taking self-inventory toward self-improvement. The individual life operates against this *7* of the year 1969 as an undercurrent. Consequently your own destiny is colored to a certain degree by this general yearly vibration of the *7.*

To what extent remains to be seen. This is revealed in the second item of the information that is required: namely, the number vibration of your own month and day of birth, which must be added to the *7* of the year.

Let's say you were born on May 5th. Add the number of the month (May is the 5th month of the year) to the number of your birthday, which is also *5:* the result is *5* plus *5,* or *10,* which reduced to a single digit becomes a *1.*

You realize, of course, that the numbers of the months are

counted beginning with January as the No. 1 month of any year.

Your next step is to add the vibrations of your birthdate (month and day), which we discovered was *1*, to the number for 1969, which we reduced to the single digit: *7*. The sum total of these numbers is *7* plus *1*, or *8*.

For example: if you were born on May 5th, you would be in an "eight" Personal Year in 1969.

When you study the meaning of the *8*, you will find that it is a year of realization. 1969 should be fruitful for those born on May 5th or any other combination that totals *1*.

THE MONTHS BY NUMEROLOGY

Month	Name	Number
1st	January	1
2nd	February	2
3rd	March	3
4th	April	4
5th	May	5
6th	June	6
7th	July	7
8th	August	8
9th	September	9
10th	October	1
11th	November	11 or 2
12th	December	12 or 3

Numerology will instruct you:
a) what to do in 1969
b) what NOT to do in 1969.

In order that you may learn the method of number analysis more rapidly we advise you to memorize two basic rules:
1) for calculating the Universal Year
2) for calculating your Personal Year.

RULE NO. 1. How to Calculate the Universal Year.
Example: 1974. Add the digits of the numbers of the year
1974 to a single number: $1+9+7+4$: totals *21*.
Reduce to a single digit: $2+1$ equals *3*.
1974 is a "Three" Universal Year.

RULE NO. 2. How to calculate your Personal Year Number:
Example: Birthday July 10th.

Add your birth month and day number: 7+1
equals *8*.

Add the *3* of the year to the *8* of the birth month
and day number. Result: 8+3 equals *11*.

The person born July 10th is in an "eleven" Personal Year
in 1974. You may interpret this as a "two."

Of course, these two rules are applicable to any current
year and any other birthdate.

But numerology has another angle you may want to learn
about and master. You can give numbers a global outlook
and judge current events by the vibrations of the universal
year, or better still by birthdates of nations.

Take a *6* for instance. It indicates adjustments: divorce or
marriage in the life of an individual, adjustments between
business partners, or generally considered between any associations. But it also pertains to the correlation between countries, in which case it forecasts war and peace, hostility or
amity between neighboring states or allied nations.

It simply amounts to this: Numerology is applicable to
the most minute personal problems of human life or to gigantic moves in the theatre of international politics.

YOUR PERSONAL YEAR

As the maestro of a popular dance band I have come to realize the value of rhythm. All is a matter of rhythm. Life is. Music is. Whether you swirl to the tune of a two-step, the vibration of the two, or when hearts thrill in a three-quarter time waltz, based on the numerical three, you will find the beat to harmonize with numbers. I could go on demonstrating the fact that rhythm and the symbols of numbers have a definite affinity.

You too may have observed how rhythm operates in your own destiny by those disconcerting ups and downs which manifest themselves from time to time. Certainly human existence does not run on an even keel, it is frequently a matter of barren years followed by a crowded hour. This principle has led to the slogan: either feast or famine. Numerology attributes this fluttering condition in life to the "Law or Periodicity." This law is not only manifest in human destiny, it also operates throughout the entire created world.

There is a definite number pattern in your own span of years. This can be mathematically computed by numbers, which will reveal your barren years when the tide is out. Then again your numbers will herald the coming of a boom in your business affairs, an upswing in career matters, or an increase of your physical attraction powers with the rosy prospect of a romance. This high-frequency in your number rhythm will advise you in advance when you may expect the "tide to come in."

This is not a matter of fortune-telling, it's plain mathematics revealed in the correlation of human factors to the cosmic pulse-beat as pictured in numbers. This has been pointedly expressed by the philosopher who stated: "Behind the warm, colorful manifestation of created life lie the glacial peaks of mathematics." No matter for what specific purpose you plan the blue-printing of your activities, it couldn't possibly be done successfully without the yardstick of numbers.

Is not our entire globe divided into the parallels of latitudes and the meridians, each tagged with its own specific number? Extend this mathematical formula into outer space and again you'll find that the celestial calculus of the vast galaxies is correlated to our own earth in the sidereal day.

Numbers are symbols. They represent values of time and energy. Your entire existence with its colorful adventures conceals, perhaps deeply hidden, this pattern of numerical precision.

These values are irrevocable and permanent. The *1* will always stand for a certain value whether applied to a letter in your name or a day in your life. It signifies a beginning, pioneering and leadership. The *2* stands for cooperation and so on. There is a pattern behind each number throughout the entire gamut of numbers from *1* to *9*.

In the Western System of Numerology the numbers *10* and *20* indicate a higher octave as a *0* is added to the one and the two respectively.

In the following pages we give you the meaning of each number from *1* to *9* in its relation to your Personal Year. You will know from your yearly number vibration where you stand in the universal pattern of life. You will be able to map out a schedule for your activities and to follow a pre-arranged plan.

We will also give you the negative aspects of each Personal Year number, so you may know what to guard against when making important decisions.

A "ONE" PERSONAL YEAR

An old Chinese proverb runs to this effect: "Even a journey of 1000 miles started with a single step." This step is your "one" year, which ushers in a cycle of nine years. Naturally, it is of highest importance that you step out into this new period of your life with the right foot and in the right direction.

This "one" Personal Year is one of beginnings. You should start something new, wander in a different groove, make departures from the past. Reconnoiter for up-to-the-minute promising business opportunities. Make contacts, worthwhile ones if possible. Widen your circle of friends and associates, including new clients or customers.

Above all fill your mind and soul with new concepts and try out untested ideas. Use original business tactics. Let a fresh wind blow around and wipe away the cobwebs of stagnant, shop-worn old methods and antiquated techniques.

When you are in a "one" Personal Year you are apt to travel and visit places that are new in your itinerary. Even if you return to localities that once were your stamping ground, you may take some sidetrips there to spots that you neglected to visit before.

A "one" Personal Year calls for initiative, originality, courage, speculative audacity. But at the same time you are advised to use your critical acumen and winnow the wheat from the chaff. Remember these "one" year conditions, for people met during that time may stick with you throughout the coming cycle of nine years. So let your choice be wise. Select friends you'd like to have around and live with through this period.

There are other tips numerology can give you on *how* to best profit by this "one" personal year. Use direct methods by shunning those go-betweens who are apt to distort your messages. Initiative should be a daily password. Go after people and things and don't take "no" for an answer. In a "one" year you may regret that you did not at least try. Be positive in all you do. Defeatism should not exist in your breviary of conduct.

Negative Aspects of a "One" Personal Year

To be that Eager Beaver who starts things with a flourish, then loses interest as soon as obstacles arise. Doing things by fits and starts. Sloppy handling of details. To make promises carelessly, then not to be able to keep them. To offend by high-pressure methods. Exaggeration of projected plans. Guard against over-optimism.

You may meet people with a strong arm who will try to bully you around. Don't let them do it. A vacillating attitude on your part when quick decision is called for. Jumping at conclusions before facts are properly gauged. Cocksureness, arrogance, self-doubt are all on the program of a negative "one" year.

Four-flushing and bluffing are taboo tactics in a "one" year and are bound to lead to failure.

Words of Wisdom from the "One" Number

Exercise self-discipline. Strengthen your will power. Be firm when you are sure you're right.

YOUR "TWO" PERSONAL YEAR

After the nerve-wracking high-frequency of the previous "one" year, you will be able to pull in your oars. Sit on the sidelines and watch for results to happen. Your strenuous efforts to get the ball a-rolling during your "one" year should now begin to manifest. At least some of the irons you've put into the fire during the last few months should show signs they've caught on; they should surely begin to glow. We already stated that you will reap in a "two" Personal Year as you have sown in the past. Now let the law of growth and development operate.

Strange as it may seem, you will find a number of desirable opportunities to surprise you during this "two" vibration. Even strokes of advantageous chances may drift your way: unexpected but favorable job offers, or advancement in your place of work. They could descend upon you like a bolt from the blue. Be receptive to such possibilities and keep your mind open to the various accumulated profits you may expect and which you rightfully deserve.

The "two" year influences are excellent for teamwork of all kind, business-wise or in career matters. Collaboration may beckon with someone who entered your life during the "one" year. Do not hesitate to tie up with newcomers. But withal, examine well their backgrounds and educational levels for the tasks you want them to do *for* you or *with* you. The "two" sometimes introduces patronage into one's destiny, someone who may take an interest in your progress. Remember then that this is an aspect when you are easily moulded into the expression of individuals met, therefore be receptive rather than creative and positive.

The "two" is propitious for collecting, for instance, accounts receivable or just plain debts. Square the ledger. Faith, patience, receptivity should win the day for you. A turning-point may drop "lucky strikes" across your pathway without any effort on your part. Therefore you should be alerted to unaccountable, agreeable surprises that are apt to push your affairs onward and upward.

Mentally and spiritually, you should unfold like a flower, for to radiate charm and to develop yourself are two of the foremost recommendations the "two" Personal Year has for you.

Negative Aspects of a "Two" Year

This vibration often shows up the defects in situations or in people, or even in your vocational equipment. Then correct shortcomings, but do not allow yourself to become discouraged. Difficulties also may be encountered in your home. Situations at the office sometimes present seemingly insurmountable barriers. But you will surely find a way out with patience and confidence in your ability. Don't make a mountain out of a molehill. You may be inclined to exaggerate minor details and let them bother you. Do not heed idle flattery.

Words of Wisdom from a "Two" Number

Cultivate self-confidence. Be yourself and stop trying to imitate others. Reach for a broadness of mind. Eliminate pettiness from your heart.

YOUR "THREE" PERSONAL YEAR

Plan some special event for this "three" Personal Year if you are artistically inclined, talented or a social leader in your community. For this delightful vibration favors projection of your personality. Bring into play your innate affability. Your motto should be: "The smile wins." Social functions are tops on the program. All forms of entertainment, professional or amateur performances, as well as radio and TV appearances, should be planned. Excellent for that debut into society, on stage, screen or the concert platform is this "three" vibration. Self-expression is recommended, be it artistic or just soberly intellectual. Pen that book, compose a song—but do something creative and beautiful.

Perhaps you function in a stodgy office atmosphere as a clerical worker or are just a housewife and the sparkle is absent from your life. Still, a message comes to you from this "three" Personal Year. Beautify yourself and your environment. Don't begrudge the dollars you may spend on new clothes. Be dapper if a male, *chic* and attractive if a woman.

Tops on a "three" program are affectional matters and social affairs. Try to be the life of the party at all times,
whether during an outdoor barbecue gathering or at a formal
function. Accept invitations and go week-ending. Mix with your
friends of both sexes and radiate cheerfulness.

Remember the adage: "Radiate and you will attract!"
Therefore have fun. Laugh and the world will seek your
company. This is not the time for gloom nor for trying to
argue with Fate. In fact, a new romance may bring spice into
your perhaps lonely existence. The "three" spells "honey-
moon." That could be a second adventure for married folk.

You will soon discover that your old inferiority complex
will vanish as you begin to put your ideas across. You will
also learn to master any kind of difficult situation with ease
as soon as you express yourself to advantage. Be more accomplished all around and ready for future opportunities.
Stand on your own feet. Follow your intuitions and do not
listen to other people or lieutenants who want to run the
show for you. This is the year to be a master of ceremonies
and to work your sense of humor. Words are a power in a
"three" vibration, therefore express yourself with a newly-
gained "small talk" eloquence.

Negative Aspects of a "Three" Year

Get rid of your aversion to entering into the spirit of gay
parties. Change your drab and colorless behavior and project
sparkle and wit. Give vent to your inner urges for fun. Go
after things that cause you happiness and will prove stimulating pastime: dancing, singing, sport events, or a congenial
game of cards.

However, if you have been that overly boisterous type who
wasted time and energy in foolish frivolities, then you'll find
this "three" year may teach you to discriminate between
worthwhile enjoyments and unprofitable diversions. Let no
circumstances lead you to engage in jobs that degrade your
prestige. Do not express in low cultural levels. Avoid extravagance.

Words of Wisdom from a "Three" Number

Cultivate a happy disposition. Follow your intuitions. Conduct yourself with dignity in public places.

YOUR "FOUR" PERSONAL YEAR

Let us state without preamble: This could be a profitable year for you from a business and educational angle, though, we admit, not from an economic one. You are endowed with a splendid sense of proportion, able to give people, situations and opportunities their proper value.

We presume that you are an average American, doing your daily chores and keeping on battling with life, valiantly. Yet a lot of things have gone wrong. What you'd planned in your "one" Personal Year evidently has been delayed, and your "three" year did not bring the cheer you had hoped it would.

Now comes your "four" Personal Year and you must take stock of yourself. This "four" year is the perfect vibration to improve your business methods and your tactics with fellow-beings. If you are an artist, inventor, composer, or somehow endowed with a creative mind, this "four" Personal Year vibration will help you to perfect your brainchild and to get it ready for the market. You may have a wonderful thing on your hands, but examine well its commercial acceptability. It may not stand muster in the light of commercial standards. You want to sell and make money? Fine! but your product must meet the competitive requirements in the field of industry. It must be market-ready, and your "four" vibration should help you to do so.

Here are some "four" key words you should remember: routine, organization, thrift, economic value. The latter applies also to your keeping house with physical energy. Some additional responsibility may be placed on your shoulders because of an illness of a co-worker, which may mean extra chores for you. Let not this duty aggravate you, for such annoying upsets are merely temporary. You will be recompensed for your cooperation at a later date.

A "four" Personal Year is not particularly a financially flush one, and the rolling dollars are often hard to catch. But there may be a bonus for work done by you that rightfully is the task of another. You may get pay for overtime work, late hours, or chores done at home for some special job. One thing is certain in a "four" vibration, you get just what you are entitled to, and perhaps not even that much.

A year for building is a "four" vibration, stressing substantiality. It is an excellent influence for detail, perfection of form, physical endurance and perseverance of morale in a humdrum job. Your application to specific tasks should be remarkable, especially in this day and age of specialization. Engineering, mechanics, technology are to the fore.

Negative Aspects of a "Four" Year

You are warned not to make a change in your job, lest you may be unemployed for quite a spell. Despondency and discouragement. Fight introversion and energy-robbing depression-moods. You may be physically depleted and have that "fagged-out feeling." Your personal magnetism is low, hence romance may prove a heartache for a while.

Words of Wisdom from a "Four" Number

Discipline yourself and your work schedules. Run your affairs on a practical timetable. Begin to write a diary and keep track of your appointments. Be orderly and systematic.

YOUR "FIVE" PERSONAL YEAR

Know this about your "five" year: The worse it starts, the better it is apt to end. For a "five" year usually brings a turning-point into your destiny. This switch in your affairs come quite unbidden, it is not solicited by you and may surprise you by its suddenness.

Therefore you are advised to keep your mind open to possible changes. Most important of all: do not plan too far ahead into your schedules. Be mentally limber like a captain ready to adjust your decisions and actions with the changes on the battlefield of life. This means: Don't sign long leases, nor affix your signature to binding agreements. You may not be able to adhere to such terms. The same is true for appointments; they may be broken at the last moment. But the "five" always compensates and sometimes an impromptu opportunity more than makes up for cancelled dates.

If you understand the law of the "five" and its pivotal nature you'll come out on top in the end. You'll discover that your original direction and your plans may be completely reversed, frequently for your ultimate good. It's because the future ahead is uncertain in a "five" year, and things you thought were blue may suddenly reveal themselves to be red.

A "five" consciousness brings intensification of practically every facet of your mental and emotional pattern. The result could be nervous tension. You should strive for calm and poise at all times in order to prevent nervous exhaustion.

Your sex appeal, too, may be rather potent and a red-hot romance is frequently on a "five" program, not always a very harmonious one we are sorry to state.

This vibration brings shift of scene, travels, unusual turning-points in job conditions, promotion or demotion as the case may be. Yet, you are warned not to change jobs of your own volition nor to leave your present residence for what you think may be a more desirable home. It isn't so, and you only will have to move again. Conditions do not last in your "five" year.

Vibrations also warn against a general partnership, or wanting to be your own boss and go into business for yourself. "Don't," says the "five," for at the close of your "five" Personal Year a most acceptable association in a business venture may be waiting for you.

That nothing lasts in a "five" year pertains also to possible disputes and "lovers' quarrels." Sharp words spoken will be explained later and reconciled in your following "six" year.

Negative Aspects of a "Five" Personal Year

So high-strung are you that irritation may lead to jumping to conclusions. False accusations often result in serious rifts. Restrain your impulse to experiment and to flit from one interest to another accomplishing nothing. Try to stay put in one place until conditions force a move upon you. Pitfalls sex-wise arise from an urge to investigate new thrills.

Words of Wisdom from a "Five" Number

Less indulgence of the "senses," but show more "sense." Freedom is a "five" word for yourself, but grant it also to others. Let your restlessness and impatience lead you to further your emotional and economic progress.

YOUR "SIX" PERSONAL YEAR

The Good Book says: "It is not good that man shall be alone!" This advice applies to women as well. That's why a "six" year should come as a welcome relief to lonely souls. You long for domesticity and companionship more than ever before. However this number favors tie-ups, both private and in business, and tends to make a home permanent. Therefore your longing for love and a congenial circle of friends is likely to be satisfied during the run of your "six" year. The affectionate side of your life should be stressed. Seek associates who share your interests and hobbies.

The "six" is a home vibration. That suggests increased obligations, especially for family members. A relative who is close to your heart or a beloved friend with whom you share a mental and spiritual affinity may play a stellar part in your life at this time.

You feel that you want to relax in your personal surroundings in a "six" year. Even if you are obliged to reside in a rented room or an apartment, you should give your environment an individual touch—things that you've gotten used to, your personal belongings, a photograph of a loved one who is absent, etc. Yes, we also find that a strongly-ruled "six" personality may acquire a pet for companionship in a "six" year. The need to exercise the affections is almost a fetish.

While the "six" influence rules your consciousness you are apt to spend much time and cash on your home. You may redecorate your residence and also your office. In order to make your home a permanent one, you may buy or build a house, acquire a farm or purchase a real estate site. It is a good real estate vibration for those who are in that line of business.

This gracious "six" vibration favors the creative artist, the talented members in the entertainment world, including those in the performing arts. Youngsters when in a "six" year often clamor to develop a talent such as dancing, playing a musical instrument, or attending a drama school. Give your kids a chance for self-expression.

But there are other prosaic impulses connected with a "six": balance the budget, sign on the dotted line, for you are likely to be in the driver's seat. No verbal agreements however. It could bring marriage or divorce, as well as adjusting partnership, associations and friendships. Straighten out your business problems or domestic troubles.

Foremost on life's ledger are human relations during this "six" year. Your psychology appears to be wise and practical, hence you operate on an even keel in matters of contacts, business-wise, social, or in private connections.

Last but not least, a mate may cross your path, sometimes miraculously so, therefore let mind and heart be receptive to the idea of affectionate expression: Object, matrimony.

Negative Aspects of the "Six" Year

Stop whining because you happen to be alone for a while. Avoid negative attitudes which lead to fault-finding of others. Curb a spirit of discontent because you're unable to keep up with the Joneses. Your display of superiority is apt to cause resentment or outright enmity. Self-righteousness and smugness are character shortcomings to guard against at this time. Don't attempt to run the lives of friends, associates or family members. Don't groan under a burden of domestic obligations. Look at the bright side of your destiny.

Words of Wisdom from a "Six" Number

Make adjustments wisely and cheerfully.

YOUR "SEVEN" PERSONAL YEAR

The "seven" is a sabbatical influence and those who can afford it should engage in a restful vacation. Your foremost psychological urge is to be alone, to get away from it all. The conventional pattern of your life will give way to the enjoyment of meditation when you escape into the sanctum sanctorum of your mind. The "seven" never favors boisterous social frivolities, or the mingling with hilarious merrymakers. Such pastimes could only prove time-robbing and would deplete your mental energy.

The desire to be sequestered from the hustle and bustle of the world is often so strong in a "seven" year that you may prefer to stay at home alone, night after night, and relax with a book or a stimulating TV stanza.

As this "seven" consciousness is introverted, it turns to self-analysis. Take stock of your essential, intrinsic worth, your mental powers, and your basic talents. You may now correct mistakes you've made in the past, or figure out ways and means to exploit more profitably your various aptitudes, vocationally or as a form of avocation. Also, you may be filled with a calm determination to achieve something worthwhile and to contribute to the spiritual advancement of your world.

The "seven" year frequently brings a delightful romantic experience, some affectionate stimulus that feeds the soul and encourages creative activities along inspirational lines. Surrounding conditions may be somewhat unconventional: social or cultural levels may not be equal; also there could be a third person in the picture as a stumbling block to a legalized set-up. This relationship may be forced to remain strictly clandestine for the duration of the "seven" influence. Later, during our "eight" stimulus, obstacles to a conventional union may be miraculously removed.

This is not a vibration for economic and business expansion, and definitely it is contrary to all forms of speculation, gambling and betting. On the other hand, the "seven" is creative, inspirational and profitable for those who engage in literary pursuits, do laboratory research work, or are of an inventive mind. While in seclusion with yourself as a channel for constructive creative inspiration, you may discover tremendously progressive new ideas.

A "seven" year sometimes brings tangible gifts—and we don't mean a bunch of posies, but unearned monies, such as inheritances, out-of-court settlements, and tokens of substantial beneficence.

Most of all, it is a splendid inducement to go on a vacation, preferably to a seashore retreat or in wild, untouched nature. It may take a cross-country trek to get there, away from noisy hotels, but you'll feel like living in paradise.

It's a year of mystery, therefore be receptive to philosphical trends, investigate occult laws, and do not close your mind to metaphysical thought. Silence should be your password, then out of the blue revelations may come.

Negative Aspects of a "Seven" Year

A warning is issued to refrain from brooding over past wrongs and injuries. Don't engage in a foolish, futile martyr complex. Don't dwell miserably over mistakes of the past and let bygones be bygones. Forgive and forget those who have offended you. See whether your own faulty psychology was not largely to blame for aggravating misunderstandings.

Words of Wisdom from a "Seven" Number

Stick to realities, but let your imagination wander into fields of beauty and harmony. Share inner riches with souls akin.

YOUR "EIGHT" PERSONAL YEAR

Have you an "eight" number prominent in your birthday? Mark this "eight" Personal Year as a milestone in your destiny from a material point of view. The "eight" is an earth number, vibrates to matter, and has a propelling reaction on your economic status if you work it right. So put your best foot forward and branch out. Expansion should head the program of your aspirations. Have faith in your ability and in the gratifying remuneration from many of the interests you've been working on during the preceding seven years of this present cycle. If hard work, sincere efforts, a practical acumen and a follow-through of your affairs have marked your tactics, rest assured you may now be in for a rewarding harvest.

It is imperative that you engage in a money consciousness at this time. Don't disdain the hard-earned dollar. Cure yourself of an attitude that "being commercial" is of secondary consideration in the pursuit to prominence and economic security. Plan projects with a "cash-in-the-pocket" objective and act accordingly.

There is a slogan which says: "It is not what you know but whom you know!" How true it is in your "eight" Personal Year you'll soon find out. Make influential contacts. Meet the top executive and not the next in line, if it is at all possible for you to do so. You will be surprised how this "eight" number will help you to get to the man at the helm. Let people and conditions work for you. Reach out for the *big* things to be done. Be alerted to *big* opportunities. Meet BIG people and act like they do: *BIG*.

Withal, the Law of Justice prevails. You will get your just reward in proportion as you have invested time and energy. But, on the other hand, be fair to others. Be grateful for favors done on your behalf. Be mindful of the lifts given you during that arduous ascent to prestige and power. Also do not overlook your assets: good health, fine business acumen, a sense of value when psychological moments for opportunity beckoned. Appreciate the happy turning-points that arose while you were climbing the rungs of the ladder to economic security.

Do not neglect the social side of your life either. Many a lucrative deal has been maneuvered on a golf course or during a pleasant week-end in a country home. Associate with those more securely situated than yourself in those social strata we just cannot afford to overlook. Politics often dominate certain business interests and they demand to be recognized.

Women when in an "eight" year frequently contract a marriage with a wealthy suitor—that eligible bachelor you've been dreaming about for some time! It seems that ulterior motives when tying the matrimonial knot are quite ethical in an "eight" Personal Year.

Negative Aspects of an "Eight" Year

Let not the "eight" consciousness deteriorate into stupid cupidity and miserliness. Avoid false pride. Cultivate tolerance, for the "eight" desire for material expansion sometimes verges on a false sense of values. Limitations of this "eight" number are your own fear complexes of dying in the poorhouse. A show-off attitude to display material wealth by a flaunting of possessions: that spectacular sport-car, the flashy mink coat, or swank country home with the Hollywood touch —the tennis court and swimming-pool. Don't try to keep up with Hollywood.

Words of Wisdom from an "Eight" Number

God made the world out of matter and substance can be a holy thing.

YOUR "NINE" PERSONAL YEAR

Some numerologists consider the "nine" year a difficult one to weather. They claim that many obstacles loom unexpectedly and block your smooth ascent to success. If you are not alerted to them, you are apt to trip and fall by the wayside. We cannot agree with such defeatism. The momentum of the "nine" is fast and furious, to be sure, but you have plenty of time beforehand to map out your objectives and act accordingly. Be prepared for emergencies; this will prevent annoying spills during your race with destiny.

The "nine" is a finishing year. It means a wind-up of your affairs that have been catching fire during the eight preceding years of this cycle. Bring things to culmination now. Force issues. Put your hand of cards upon the table and declare your intentions. If you find insurmountable hurdles to tumble across your way and block your progress hopelessly, then you should remember the other key-word of the "nine": *elimination.*

Cast from your destiny the superfluous and the undesirable. This includes time-robbing activities, futile experimentations, and hobbies and pastimes that drain energy and get you nowhere.

The same is true for those boring acquaintances that have proven themselves hangers-on, encroaching on your time and energy and contributing nothing in return, either physically or spiritually. Economically, they have been a complete drain, for you have nothing in common with such so-called friends any more, not even a congenial game of Bridge. Eliminate people who get in your hair. Hobbies that once proved pleasurable but no longer relax nor stimulate you should be scratched from your roster.

But elimination can also be physical: getting that obnoxious molar extracted, your eye-glasses adjusted. Maybe a minor operation has been recommended by your physician for some time, so you should no longer struggle against the inevitable. Remember the "nine" Personal Year is excellent for a complete overhauling of your organism.

The "nine" is a top vibration for publicity, advertising, promotion, public appearances and that discreet ballyhoo you now could use effectively with your worth to impress the boss, supervisor or even your husband or wife. A good time to blow your own horn whenever advisable!

Make an inventory of what you want and what you do not want, then focus your mind on the direction you should take to promote success.

Last but not least, "nine," being of a universal vein, often instills a desire to see the world. No better number for globe-trotting and venturing forth into foreign lands than this "nine" vibration.

Negative Aspects of a "Nine" Year

Too scattery. Wasteful of energy and money. Too many irons in the fire due to poor judgment and lack of proper discrimination. Your tactics with people should not be lackadaisical. Remember the Shakespearan adage: Neither a borrower nor a lender be.

Words of Wisdom from a "Nine" Number

Be impersonal in your conduct with individuals. Have that global viewpoint on specific interests, in business or in national economics.

YOUR PERSONAL MONTH
AND DAY

You may want to know more than just the pattern of your Personal Year. A certain month in 1970, for instance, is marked with red in your calendar of special dates. Some very important event may loom, such as examinations in school, a law-suit and appearances in court, or a residential removal. You may want to find out how to conduct yourself during a vital interview, or more, you wish to select a propitious day for this engagement. What should your attitude be? What should you say, or better still, what should you avoid saying? Maybe a day set for a certain event is altogether ill-timed and you may want to change it to a more propitious day. Therefore you should calculate the number value of this particular month and day in 1970.

Let's stick to the birthdate May 5th. An important event is planned for March 7th. What numerical month and day would this be for one born May 5th?

You already calculated the Personal Year number for this birthday, which was 9. Now you must add to this 9 the number of the month of March, which is 3, and reduce the total to a single digit, as follows:

Nine plus 3 equals 12; reduce to 3. You will find this month rather propitious for one born May 5th, that is from a personality angle.

For the "three" is suitable for any event which calls for the projection of the personality and an affable manner when meeting individuals or the public. The latter includes personal appearances from stage or in a concert hall, public speaking, or even for conventions and important business conferences, or as in our example, an interview.

March is favorable for one born May 5th. But even then a day not suitable for an interview may pop up in his calendar of a generally propitious period. The man born May 5th is anxious to select a good day for this interview in relation to his own Personal Year number, which is "nine."

The appointment has been set for March 7th, 1970. What sort of day would it be for one born May 5th?

Here is the rule:

Add the number of the Personal Month to the vibration of the calendar day, which is 7 (March 7).

It adds up to this: 3 plus 7 equals 10.

Reduce 10 to a single digit: which is 1.

Therefore, March 7 is a "one" day in a "three" month for a May 5th birthday.

The interview should have gratifying results. This day is well timed for any undertaking requiring originality and singleness of purpose. It also suggests a new approach to some perhaps timeworn problem, a valuable asset when presenting new ideas.

Numbers further advise this person to be positive in his statements, on this "one" day, not to be wishy-washy about his bearing or delivery. He should stick to plain facts, and he will find that this date will become a milestone in his career.

We advise you to learn the following numerology rules:

YOUR PERSONAL MONTH

Add the number of your Personal Year to the number of the calendar month. Reduce the total to a single digit.

Example

The birthday is July 10th. The month for the event is April, 1974.

Add the number of July, 7, to the birthday, 10 (1) to his Personal Year number, which is "eleven." (You obtained this by adding the month and day of birth to the calendar year number.)

The calendar year number of 1974 is: 1 plus 9 plus 7 plus 4, total: 21, reduce to 3, 1974 is a "three" Universal Year.

The number of the calendar month April is 4. Now add the person's Personal Year number, "eleven," to the calendar month number 4: total is 6. A man born July 10th, is in a "six" Personal Month in April, 1974.

YOUR PERSONAL DAY

Now what about this man's Personal Day for April 15, 1974?

Add the Personal Month number for April, which was "six," to the calendar day, which is *15*, reduced to *6*. It totals *12*, reduced to *3*.

This man's Personal Day is "three" for April 15, 1974, if he was born on July 10th.

When interpreting the monthly or daily personal numbers you must proceed deductively, that is from the general to the specific. This means that the Personal Year number dominates the nature of your Personal Month, or your Personal Day influences.

Let's say you are in a "one" Personal Month, but your Personal Year is "eight." Then judge your month in relation to the "eight" of your Personal Year. It would indicate taking the initiative (*1*) in solving financial problems (*8*).

If the Personal Year is a "seven," however, it would suggest that you lay plans in secrecy (*7*) without revealing them at *this* time. In other words, your Personal Month and your Personal Day are modified by your Personal Year number.

A "ONE" MONTH

Take the initiative in contacting people or trying to bring favorable conditions about. Use the telephone whenever possible. Direct communications are advised. Tackle your neglected correspondence. Be alert to unexpected new propositions, but examine well all offers. Call on customers. Go after new clients. Be cheerful, dynamic, positive. This is a good time for trying out new ideas. Be sure you're right before swinging into action. Follow through on all contacts made. Discard undesirable or futile newcomers later. If new propositions involve shift of scene, even long journeys, by all means investigate their future possibilities.

NEGATIVE: Foolish obstinacy. Argumentativeness. Indolence. Indifference. Discouragement.

A "ONE" DAY

You should be filled with a self-starter spirit and should get busy along lines of constructive activity. Check first on your

Personal Year influences and follow through on interests indicated by its number. If an *8*, finances and economics; if a *6*, adjustments. Main thing: be self-reliant and have faith in your ability and vocational qualifications. Follow your hunches. Seek advancement in your job. Ask for favors—that bonus or raise in salary if circumstances warrant this gesture. Originate a new plan. A departure from previous tactics may be advisable.

Look over the list of your creditors and offer more lenient terms. Fine for starting on a new foot into untried ventures. Branch out. Expand your sphere of prestige.

NEGATIVE: Curb irritability. Impatience accomplishes nothing in a "one" day. You may be apt to be over-anxious, then remember that high-pressure sales tactics may kill your opportunities. Test your methods as to their practical wisdom. Display calm determination. Curb tendency to worry. Let no one but in, and obey the voice of your intuitions.

A "TWO" MONTH

Be relaxed but alert, no matter what problems may come up. Let important issues approach *you*, then react according to your intuitions. If problems arise, consult friends, relatives or specialists in the field of your troubles. This month is fine for negotiation and for establishing friendly relations where friction existed. Don't bulldoze your way through finicky situations. Be tactful. Socialize with stimulating friends. Do not force issues. Recharge your worn nerve-batteries by resting whenever time permits. Look for a practical, sensible way out of puzzling situations.

NEGATIVE: Discouragement. Indulging in gloom and moodish tantrums. Gossip. Dissatisfaction with self and your destiny. Envy and jealousy may plague your mind.

A "TWO" DAY

Good for self-effacement and being a good listener. Keep your own personality subdued. Consult others about their opinions. Attend to details of projects started on your "one" day. Be a mixer, but don't want to run the show. Gather news, and informaion about specific propositions. Take inventory of your prospects, classify opportunities. Good for pigeon-holing your future possibilities. Ferret out facts. Play second fiddle, and be willing to be the accompanist.

NEGATIVE: Avoid causing friction by wanting to have it your own way. Whining. Pestering others with your troubles. Don't wear a scowl on your face. Stop belly-aching. Don't judge others by appearances that could be misleading.

A "THREE" MONTH

Unless your yearly vibrations conflict, like a "four" or a "seven" year, you should have an enjoyable time in your "three" month. Plan some special social function or engagements and appearances that will further your popularity and interests. (Entertain with parties and be entertained. Accept invitations.) The artistically inclined person could go in for exhibits, fashion shows, public showings, and projection of some talent from the platform. Philanthropical parties should go over big this month. Main thing: project your personality to advantage.

NEGATIVE: Wasteful spending of cash. Foolish frivolities. Indulgences of senses. Indiscriminate statements. Giving offense by a show-off behavior.

A "THREE" DAY

What would be better for self-expression than a number that boosts personality and offers an occasion which calls for an effervescent atmosphere? You should be like a soldier of fortune, drift with the happy current and refuse to worry. Take the bad with the good and like it. The outer appearance should score. Dress up. Be dapper. Good for presenting yourself in interviews, while soliciting a job, or calling on friends.

Fine for shopping. You will be surprised over your excellent taste and judgment of values. Smile in the face of seeming frustrations. A "three" day could bring a Pollyanna influence.

NEGATIVE: Scattering of your forces. Brooding over a bleak future. Defeatism. Anxiety over money matters. Distrust of people. Inferiority complex.

A "FOUR" MONTH

Your personal magnetism may be low, so do not count on carrying a touchy situation with the flourish of your personality. Hard facts count. A time to apply yourself to detail, and specific tasks. Humdrum routine. Classifying, filing, paying of bills. Investigate past efforts and see where corrections or improvements are due. The "four" is related to menial labor—and you may plan that do-it-yourself Simonizing job on the family car, or working in your garden. Corrections, proofreading of important letters, mechanical labor, all are suitable for this month. Main thing: build substantiality.

NEGATIVE: Lack of enthusiasm. Laziness. Sloppy handling of detail. Upsetting routine organizations. Moroseness. Fretting over health conditions.

A "FOUR" DAY

A routine day for adhering to a rigid schedule. Apply yourself from morn to midnight to whatever tasks you have mapped out for your "four" day. Keep an eye on the clock and get things done according to schedule. Attend to balancing your budget, cleaning out desk drawers, mending the wardrobe, and checking your wardrobe. Attend to some of the odd jobs you've put off for some time—all these cumbersome tasks should head the list of your working plan. Economy should rule the day. A good day to fast.

NEGATIVE: Don't splurge by foolish display of dollars. Be frugal. Lack of system could be costly. Extravagance. Slovenly mismanagement.

A "FIVE" MONTH

The pivotal nature of the "five" is bound to manifest itself, so why try to follow a rigid itinerary during this month? Be mentally alert and pliable of decision. Adjust your plans with the changes that arise unexpectedly. Better attend to things that are inspirational and unsolicited. Fine for promotion, advertising, and expansion as the need for it arises. Nerves may be jittery, so look out for sharp words. Ambiguity of speech may mar relationships. If misunderstandings arise in your "five" month, they will be reconciled later on. Nothing is permanent now, least of all your sentimental status. Emotions fluctuate in a "five" period. Love affairs may blow hot and cold and have little promise of permanency. Things you start now are not apt to last. Broken engagements may upset you. Don't take them seriously, for a more attractive, yet unexpected, date may be waiting for you around the corner. Don't aim for static conditions this month.

NEGATIVE: Indulgences of the senses. Wasting energy in futile, time-robbing pleasures. Lack of organization. Chaos in your affairs. A confused mind that leads to indecision.

A "FIVE" DAY

Excellent for mingling with people, for your attraction powers are pleasantly enhanced. Select places where you could meet strangers. Variety is the password of this day, so do something original, depart from stagnant ruts. Let "difference" rule your choice of activities or diversions. Try out something utterly novel and unique. Get away from clichés. Let opportunities approach you, then investigate their merit.
NEGATIVE: Irritability. Militant attitudes. Nervous tension. Jumping at conclusions. Bluntness of speech. Impulsive statements and hasty actions. Quarrelsome. Look out for accidents.

A "SIX" MONTH

Apply the principle of beauty to your home as you applied it to your personal self in your "three" influence. For domesticity and adjustments with associates and relatives are now heading the list of your special interests. Therefore plan some family reunion or visit to relatives. This month also favors marriage, if the occasion arises, as well as matrimonial adjustments—perhaps a divorce. Members of different generations call for attention, elders as well as children, your own or someone else's. A propitious vibration is this "six" also for socializing, and for contacting friends whom you may have unwillingly neglected. Get in touch with acquaintances you haven't cultivated for some time.

If some domestic obligations come up, attend to them cheerfully. Pay attention to your surroundings, beautify your home. Additionally you may pay some attention to your special talents, or indulge in hobbies—music, the arts, the dance, the theatre, something that will stimulate your mind.
NEGATIVE: Unwillingness to adjust either in domestic or matrimonial difficulties. Partnership adjustments also may be due. Shoulder responsibilities. Get out of the old rut.

A "SIX" DAY

Meet responsibilities that are justly your share: Entertain and be entertained. Members of the family should be cultivated. Make a call to a hospital, or a sickbed. Bring a gift. Improve and beautify your surroundings. Have a conciliatory attitude toward those who have offended you. Bear no grudges, for you too may have given offense.

NEGATIVE: Writing letters of complaint. Causing friction by an "I'd rather be right" attitude. Be cooperative. Adjust with partners. Avoid nagging. Don't be hypercritical of others, throw stones.

A "SEVEN" MONTH

Tackle nothing new, but attend to the business at hand. Receptivity and passiveness accomplish more than aggressive self-assertion. Watch health, metabolism may be sluggish. Hence a diet free from fats and condiments is advised. A good time to go on a vacation. Your intitutions run high and your analysis may be almost perfect. A good month to plan future activities. Fine for invention, creativity, writing. Silence and patience should be your motto. Self-analysis is favored. Examine your affairs as to their practicability, and lay plans when to swing into action.

NEGATIVE: Reaching out for financial gain. Speculation could be disappointing. Being impatient with results or with people. Don't indulge in a martyr complex. Being overly suspicious.

A "SEVEN" DAY

Above all don't hurry, and remember: "Take it easy." This could be a day of revelations, both intellectually, along lines of creativity, as well as spiritually. Relax. Your intuitive insight should be remarkable. Fine for associating with a few congenial souls. Entertainment should be stimulating, but on a high cultural level. A day for seclusion, to get away into the country away from city noises. "Seven" is a water element number, hence sailing, fishing or a trip to the seashore are advised.

NEGATIVE: To hasten and hurry. To seek pleasures of the senses. Alcoholism. Impatience. Intolerance. Rush methods of transportation—auto-speeding and flying—could be critical this day.

AN "EIGHT" MONTH

Turn your mind to practical and economic problems.

Make bank deposits. Check your bank account. Call business meetings and conferences, or attend them. Solidify your economic security. Try to improve fiscal status. Be cognizant of your power and try to excel in whatever you do. Do jobs better than the other man. Speculation and investments are recommended. Expand and improve finances or lay plans of how to accomplish this. Good for selling and putting property or merchandise on the market. Attend to legal technicalities. Apply for a patent or copyright. Submit your brainchild to publishers or producers if the circumstances demand it.

NEGATIVE: Being fearful over lack of money. Displaying insufficient vision and practical acumen. Your fiscal judgment is poor. Intolerance. Being unfair or unjust to others. Abusive of underlings. Extravagance because of your own improvidence. Complete absence of a sense of economic value.

AN "EIGHT" DAY

Concentrate on business, or your financial affairs and on how to improve your earning capacity. If an opportunity arises to better yourself materially, grasp it quickly. Do not turn down offers because you're wanting in courage. Help yourself by helping others. Solicit interviews with bosses, superiors or with important personages. Make a bank loan, or a bank deposit according to your circumstances. Good for soliciting a better job. Take a chance money-wise. Think of ways and means of how you could make those extra dollars count.

NEGATIVE: Indolence. Hoarding of dollars instead of putting them to good use. Underestimating your own ability. Not properly exploiting yourself.

A "NINE" MONTH

This is a difficult month to weather, for the eliminative influences often introduce losses of personal belongings into your life. They may also bring a loss because of petty pilfering, or absent-mindedness. Carry little cash on your person.

Avoid friction with loved ones, for a rift at this time may be permanent. On the other hand, this is a good aspect for eliminating people or undesirable conditions from your affairs.

Cultivate a broad outlook on conditions. An impersonal attitude is recommended in your relation with individuals. Do not hold on to things or people who are about to drift from your sphere; for your destiny pattern shows a realignment in your relationships and associations.

NEGATIVE: A sense of self-righteousness. Laying too great importance on personal feelings. Avoiding service to a cause or to humanity.

A "NINE" DAY

A day for finishing things rather than starting them. A wind-up day. Be careful of losses, missing objects are not likely to be retrieved. Cultivate group consciousness. Reach out for the public rather than for the individual. Public appearances, self-expression along artistic lines, publicity, promotion are favored. Shift of scene may prove relaxing: automobiling, vacationing, a pleasant trip. A sales vibration in order to get rid of superfluous possessions.

NEGATIVE: Hesitancy. Carelessness. Indolence. Timidity in crowds, shrinking from human contacts.

II

Your Path of Destiny

THE LAW OF RELATIVITY applies to numerology as to everything else in life. You already know that your Personal Month and Day must be judged in relation to your Personal Year number. But this in turn cannot be fully evaluated unless it is related to your Path of Destiny influence. This is basic, for it is computed from your complete birthday: month, day and year. You may change your name during the span of your lifetime, but you certainly cannot ever alter the day on which you were born. That is permanent, no matter how much you may fib about your birth year.

YOUR DESTINY NUMBER

In the previous part of this book you learned how to calculate your Personal Year influence, as well as those of your Personal Month and Day. These factors were based upon your month and day of birth only, but your year of birth was not drawn into consideration. Now you must add the sum-total of your year of birth, reduced to a single digit, to your month and day numbers. Therefore your Path of Destiny is calculated from your birth month, birth day and birth year, three numerical factors in all, which must be reduced to a single digit.

This is a basic aspect and reflects the pattern of your destiny, for which reason it is also called your Path of Life.

Example

The birthdate is: March 26, 1932.

March is the 3rd month of the year—value: *3*

The 26th day of the month must be reduced. *2+6* equals *8.*

The year value is: *1+9+3+2* equals *15*, reduce to *6.*

Now you must add the total: *3+8+6* equals: *8.*

Conclusion: The Path of Destiny of the birthdate: March 26, 1932, is *8.*

RULE

How to find your Path of Destiny number:

It is based upon your birthdate, the sum-total of your month, day and year of birth. Add these numbers and reduce them to a single digit.

What does the Path of Destiny number indicate?

It suggests the reason for which you came on earth, how you can develop yourself and what you should do.

What Your Path of Destiny Number Signifies

A challenge is involved. You are called upon to master certain conditions in your life, and your Destiny Number will acquaint you with the nature of this challenge. You must strive to live up to the call of what this number represents.

A "1" PATH OF DESTINY

It is best that you start from scratch and learn to stand on your own feet, no matter how complicated a psychological problem or an economic hurdle may be. You should be at the helm, make your own decisions, regardless of the fact that you may have counsellors and advisors. Do not rebel against responsibilities placed upon your shoulders. Try to establish new standards, new methods and originate your own tactics. It is a mistake if you follow the beaten path, unless it is the only sensible and practical road open to you. When you pioneer unknown territories, and that could be in the commercial realm, or when you do research work and experiment, come to your own practical or scientific conclusions. It is best not to repeat yourself. Meet your challenge and be a leader, but select your own helpers and assistants for minor positions. Above all do not allow a Smart Aleck to butt into your affairs.

A "2" PATH OF DESTINY

Yours is a challenge by negation, for diplomacy, tact, poise and suavity are required of you, rather than aggressive self-assertion. Learn to play second fiddle. You win by using your innate psychological know-how in handling underlings, family members or business associates. When you demonstrate your exemplary cooperation, you will master environment and groups of people without friction. You should tread the beaten path, wander business avenues that have been tested, and let those with a pioneer spirit map out progressive ideas for you. Mistakes you make are usually those of your predecessors in any given vocational position, but you are wise to correct them. You should go through life with little trouble if you use these peaceful, conciliatory tactics.

A "3" PATH OF DESTINY

Self-expression is the password your Destiny number decrees. You should bring sparkle and joy into your environment, bolster up the morale of others by your effervescent personality. Early in life train yourself to see an optimistic aspect in troublesome situations. When you meet up with negative thinkers, try to convert them to a hopeful outlook on their problems. This can best be achieved by a friendly, cheerful and encouraging attitude on your part. You may soon discover that you have a gift of being a good mixer, therefore cultivate friendships and hold them on a level keel by demonstrating patience and diplomacy. To try and dominate others would be a mistake. Bring cheer by using any talent you may have developed. Cultivate associations. Try to be the life of a party when mingling with merrymakers.

A "4" PATH OF DESTINY

This is a cornerstone number and without this "Temple Four-Square," there could be no progress in life. For your Destiny Number demands of you to show the world the value of the "sweat of the brow": attention to detail, ability to schedule routine jobs and to apply yourself to humdrum tasks. "Duty" is your middle name, so why chafe under the burden of obligations? Understand that your destiny number is not that of a gambler or get-rich-quick schemer. But economic security could be yours by shrewd accumulation of possessions and savings. Learn to value the form aspects of created ideas, of inventions and products launched upon the open markets. Stand on your two feet and come down to earth in any new undertakings you may help to launch. You operate best from a fixed anchorage. By reaching out for worthwhile opportunities that are not transitory, you will soon build lasting benefits for yourself.

A "5" PATH OF DESTINY

This 5, being a pivotal number, teaches you to be pliable to the vicissitudes of life: be prepared for quick and frequent changes, unexpected turning-points, shifts of scene, and many travels in vocational interests. Do not get moored to a fixed anchor, but reach out for the freedom of sudden changes in your home environment. These are usually caused by the varied aspects of your affairs. It would pay you to learn foreign languages and to handle people of different nationalities or races than your own. Be alert to new opportunities and adaptable to unusual circumstances. By seeking unique and untried ventures you will soon find that experience pays off in the end. Learn to do two or more things at the same time and demonstrate ingenuity when tackling various angles of business projects. Your innate sense of humor and mental adaptability should help you overcome the barriers of opposing factions.

A "6" PATH OF DESTINY

When you realize that the meaning of your Destiny number is *adjustment*, you will soon begin to dovetail with others in meeting responsibilities of almost any kind, in private life or in your business or professional set-up. Your task is to meet inharmonious conditions head-on and begin to adjust them. This also pertains to opposite viewpoints and to understand the other fellow's angle of approach to life. Be a negotiator, a peacemaker, and adjuster when difficulties arise in your own life as well as in the lives of others. See points of harmony where hostility exists and try to persuade others to meet on friendly ground. That implies the advice never to use force but to employ amicable methods. These principles of bringing constructive conditions into groups of varied factions could be extended by you into community interests, club activities, and philanthropic functions. You should generally demonstrate the enthusiasm and spirit of a do-gooder.

A "7" PATH OF DESTINY

"Sitting on the side-lines" is the essence of this so-called sabbatical number. To delve into hidden truths—even to ferret out facts like a detective—to take time out for mental analysis and to cultivate the spirit of a counsellor is the task demanded of you as a destiny challenge. No wonder the 7 has been called the number of the priest and the philosopher. For you must concern yourself with increasing your spiritual wisdom and the store of your practical knowledge. This is not a material influence, but somehow economic opportunities beckon when least expected. You seem to be economically protected by some mysterious twist of fate. Learn the value of silence. Take time out to rest and relax, to ponder on spiritual laws, and to apply them to your practical affairs in every day problems. Partnerships should be taken with a grain of salt. To hasten and hurry would mean for you to run into complications if not serious trouble. Take it easy. Learn to be alone and like it.

AN "8" PATH OF DESTINY

This is a material influence, one of power through accumulation of wealth or the handling of finance. Therefore you should strive to work harmoniously with organized groups, private enterprises on a large scale or even government departments. Remember always that prosperity and economic progress combine to make your 8 Destiny Path a successful one, and you should endeavor to tie up with power groups. The business realm and commercial activities are your best bet vocationally. Imagination is not your long suit as a rule but efficiency, managerial skill, and executive ability could be developed by you through occupational experiences. Do not scoff at the fact that "cash" and financial capital represent power in our present economic system. Understand such laws of economics and do not abuse them.

A "9" PATH OF DESTINY

"Culmination" is usually a by-word applied to this Path of Destiny number, because your job would be to see projects through to a successful conclusion, although they may have hung fire for some time. But there is another side to this 9 influence, namely its global aspects and the universality we associate with national or international movements. Cultivate a global outlook, develop interests in current events issues beyond your hometown. Expand your mental horizon. It would also help your progress if you were to associate yourself with humanitarian soceieties and thereby serve a good cause. Lift yourself out of ruts, elevate your viewpoint from your own petty problems and difficulties to a wider sphere of interests. This is not a money number. Your talents and vocational aptitudes are geared toward handling business mechanism, promotion and personnel rather than the cash register. But somehow you seem to be divinely protected economically.

AN "11" PATH OF DESTINY

This is a master-number and if it happens to be your destiny influence, you may reduce it to a single digit and interpret it as a "2." Read, therefore, what has been said about a 2 Path of Life.

But if you have reached a superior position in life or are aiming to do so, you may want to meet the challenge of the *11* in its hyper-potential aspects. This indicates that many finicky situations must be met, even subtle underhandedness and covered-up hostile opposition to your plans. Cultivate philosophical discrimination in order to be able to look through such schemes, and let not glib "smoothies" put one over on you. Your life may not be of the humdrum variety, probably because you are a specialist in a certain field of endeavor which calls for a pattern that needs constant adjustments. Learn to trust your intuitions. Your originality and inventiveness must be steered into practical channels if you expect profitable harvests from them. Philosophy and mysticism may cross your life path unexpectedly. Embrace unusual trends of thought. You should benefit by such philosophical attitudes toward life.

A "22" PATH OF DESTINY

You may reduce this double number to a *4* and follow the advice given in the paragraph of a *4* Destiny Path. The *22* is a power-number, namely a *4* on a higher octave.

But if you decide that a *22* influence dovetails with your particular occupational aspirations, you may as well learn to adapt yourself to a universal scope on a constructive plane. This is a master-number and the picayune harassments of daily living should be put on the top shelf. Instead learn to function *big*, to think with a broad mind and work with large, preferably national or international, organizations. Political insitutions, the world theatre of commerce and ideologies, and movements that feature philanthropy and world peace are a background against which you may function successfully. Be an idealist. Radiate positive, cheerful emotions, extend love toward humanity and cultivate tolerance and harmony. Select a vocation that calls for super-specialization. Many innovators of new movements in art, science and philosophy have followed the master-number *22* to ultimate fame and fortune.

YOUR LIFE CYCLES

According to the fundamental teachings of numerology, the span of human existence is composed of three major cycles, each with a number value of its own.

These three cycles are:

The FIRST or formative cycle, based on the numerical value of the birth *month*.

The SECOND period is the middle cycle, actually the major one. It carries the number of the *day* of birth reduced to a single digit. It is the productive cycle of human existence.

The THIRD or last, but by no means the least, cycle is the final sunset period in the life of a man or woman. It's the harvest cycle and is based on the number of the birth *year*, reduced to a single digit.

Here is an example:

CHARLES LINDBERGH was born on February 4, 1902. When broken down numerologically, his birthday results in the following number pattern.

$$\frac{\text{February}}{2} \quad \frac{4}{4} \quad \frac{1902}{3} \quad \text{total: } 9.$$

You will recall that the number *2*, which determines the conditions in his first or formative cycle, has affinity with the female side of humanity. This is borne out in Lindbergh's destiny, in that he was a widow's son and that his mother was the motivating influence which moulded his formative years. The "mother" influence is signified by the *2* of his first cycle.

The *4* is the significator of technology, mechanics and science. It is therefore numerologically explained why the *4* represents the productive years in the life of this famous aviator.

The *4* certainly is a tester. It is not a frivolous or fun provoking ray, but introduces grave human experiences into the life. This is illustrated by the gruesome experience of the kidnapping of his firstborn son, and the tragic death of this infant. The notoriety following on the heels of this famous criminal case resulted in the Lindbergh Law, ruling the death penalty for kidnappers. All of this is indicated by the *4* middle cycle as well as by the universal *9* of his destiny number. The *9* is a global influence and was there anything more sensational than the news of the "Lindbergh baby" abduction, which flashed around the world.

The last cycle of Lindbergh's numberscope, represented by the *3*, is the most pleasant of all numbers, and we may well presume that this famous aviator will have time and leisure to indulge in the hobbies and pleasurable activities which are satisfying to his soul. This is one of the nicest last cycles to experience.

You may wonder where in this number pattern are the indications for accumulated affluence on a financial plane. The *4* has an unfortunate connotation of making the remuneration from personal vocational efforts rather disappointing. Quite true, but don't forget that the Colonel wrote a book which was a best seller. Later it was made into a motion picture for which he reputedly received a fee in seven digits. This was his income from a sideline.

Now look at his Path of Destiny *9*. Frequently you find that such persons get a substantial income from an activity that was once a hobby, or sideline, and later became a major factor in their economic supply.

Cycle Pattern
Your Three Major Life Cycles
EXAMPLE: October 14, 1890
(Ex-President Eisenhower)

FIRST CYCLE: *Month: October* 10, reduce to *1*.
The first life cycle is called:
The Formative Cycle 1

SECOND CYCLE: *Day:* 14, reduce to *5*.
This second or middle cycle is called:
The Cycle of Productivity 5

THIRD CYCLE: *Year:* 1890. Reduce to *9*.
The last cycle is called:

The Harvest Cycle   9

Total of numbers *15*
Reduce 15: (*1* plus *5*)   6

Ex-President Eisenhower's Path of Destiny number is symbolized by the 6.

The Path of Life influences in the case of Mr. Eisenhower are symbolized by the number 6, which represents the adjuster and the peacemaker. It is quite evident that Eisenhower's constant endeavor has been toward preventing another frightful bloody holocaust, of which he has sampled two major ones.

This number also means to comfort those in need and to offer asylum to political refugees. It accounts for the innumerable foreign Displaced Persons who found shelter in the U.S.A. during the Eisenhower Administration. This influence can well be called a "cosmic guardian" of the underdogs in human society.

And it is an excellent ray to work with others, an essential both of the militaire and the politician, "6" ruled persons do *not* like to work alone.

YOUR FORMATIVE CYCLE

This life cycle comprises your childhood, the education you may have received, and the cultural level of your parental home, against which your first formative years were spent. It also includes the influences of your sisters and brothers, of playmates and school companions; in fact, of the entire human conglomeration you contacted then, even grandparents, uncles and aunts, foster parents, neighbors or chance acquaintances.

Here is where the Science of Numbers agrees with the modern psychologist: your early contacts have a definite formative influence on the development of your character.

The educational standards, such as grammar school training which is a requisite for all youngsters, high-school, and college years of academic learning, perhaps special training in the crafts or in skilled labor constitute the tools you learned to handle in your youth in order to qualify you for the struggle of existence.

This first, or formative, cycle is represented by the number of your month of birth, judged in relation to your Path of Destiny aspect.

Numerology teaches a successive stepping up of cyclic potency from one life period to another. That means as you have exploited the possibilities of your first cycle so may you be able to function—successfully or otherwise—in the following one, the Cycle of Productivity. Then the matured man and woman take their places in society, either to reach prominence, perhaps fame, or merely to operate in a limited sphere of activity and in a narrow environment.

According to your cyclic number vibration your early life could be tranquil and harmonious, sheltered by love and understanding, when talents could be developed. Or against a turbulent environment the tender child soul may be bruised and the character blighted. In such cases, talents and vocational aptitudes are not sufficiently developed, with the result that the true nature of the youngster suffers from repression complexes. These are difficult to shake and often leave their mark on the character as a barrier to true happiness and contentment with one's existence.

Then, too, there are cases of premature exploitation of a talent, in the case of the child prodigy. Little Shirley Temple (born April 23rd) and Jackie Coogan are examples of amazing projection of personality in early childhood and the ability to work in an artistic or commercial realm, with considerable material profits.

The immortal composer Mozart (born January 27, 1756) was a tiny tot when performing on the piano at the Imperial Court of Vienna. He was so little that a cushion had to be placed on his chair and the pedals had to be raised, so his feet could reach them. Yet he played with brilliance and singular musical maturity. Felix von Mendelssohn (born February 3, 1809) is another musician who composed his electrifying score for Shakespeare's *A Midsummer Night's Dream* before he had reached his twentieth year, but in his second cycle of productivity his genius rapidly declined.

These are exceptions to the rule, of course, but the numberscopes show an overwhelming urge for self-expression of an inherent talent in a formative stage of development.

YOUR CYCLE OF PRODUCTIVITY

This is based on your day of birth and is the most vitally important period in human existence. It shows your sphere of influence in the society wherein you operate, and what type of work would be most profitable and gratifying for you, judged by the influence of this cycle in correlation with the pattern of your Path of Life aspect.

In a following chapter we give you a description of what the numbers of each day of the month from 1 to 31 signify. You may find your occupational guide according to your cycle number in this list of vocational suggestions.

Here are general rules you should first apply when studying your Cycle of Productivity influences.

Are your cycles stepping up from a lower to a higher number?

Mozart was born in a *1* first cycle, and leaped from there into a 27 day of birth, indicating that his second cycle was ruled by a 9 (2+7=9). That jump represents the span of all numbers from *1* to *9*. He exploited his number pattern to the fullest, for he reached fame during his lifetime, acclaim by his contemporaries, and ultimate immortality in the history of music.

But this jump was also performed by Al Capone, the notorious gangster of the Prohibition era. He was born on January 18. This represents a *1* childhood period and a 9 middle cycle influence, again a leap through the arc of numbers. He became a power in the underworld, handling countless sums of money, ruling like a despotic potentate over the members of gangsterland. However, all his energies were directed against society. He fought established principles and laws by his ruthless pursuit of criminal codes.

Know, then, that your numberscope does not indicate the spiritual development of the ego, whether you live on a high plane in evolution and strive to reach even higher levels. There are cases of degradation also when the cresent of human achievements curves downward and plunges into ever lower strata of the social system.

President Eisenhower's birthdate also has *1* for his first cycle (born in October). He stepped ahead when he reached his *5* Cycle of Productivity (born on the 14th day of the month). His third life cycle is represented by a 9 (birthyear, 1890). So you see, there is a continuous climb, from *1* through *5* to an ultimate 9, and no one can say that this famous statesman did not make the grade of his number challenge.

There are downward steps too. Lindbergh progressed from a *2* (February) into a *4* (birthday), and now experiences a *3* for his third life cycle. This shows plainly that the big things in his life were accomplished during his second cycle, and that his third one promises an enjoyment of the fruits of his labors.

When analyzing your second cyclic number, you should pay attention to the fact of its so-called "gender." Is this number an *even* one or an *uneven* one? The even number usually indicate the opportunity of harmonious partnerships or associations. The uneven numbers in a second cycle advise that you operate as a lone eagle, or as one in a group, perhaps one in a set-up of three or more associates. But a general 50-50 partnership is successful only in rare instances with a *1, 3, 5, 7, 9* or *11* number for your middle cycle. When the Path of Destiny number reveals a strong partnership influence, it could mitigate the indications of your middle cycle aloneness in action.

Please turn to the chapter on the birthday numbers and what they represent in your Cycle of Productivity.

YOUR HARVEST CYCLE

This is the day and age of Social Security, when free men and true are supposed to retire at the age of 65 and do little or nothing. And the fair ones have an edge on the males, with a 62-year deadline. Then they are expected to concentrate on nothing more than the pots and pans.

This dovetails to a certain extent with the cyclic rhythm of human existence, but at no time does numerology decree that people in their sixties should sit by the sidelines and just loaf. It is a harvest cycle, to be sure, when some form of income could be enjoyed, but activity in one way or another is not excluded.

Nearly everyone we know in this age bracket is busy with some interest or other from which a gratifying income is derived. And when we glance at the pages of history we find that many had reached their peak after their sixtieth year.

Here are a few Titans of fame who were busy to their last day, even as octogenarians. Take the famous symphony conductor Arturo Toscanini, born March 25, 1867, whose genius did not diminish and who was able to stand up well under the nervous strain of personal appearances.

John D. Rockefeller, Sr., attended to all his multiple interests, managed a huge organization personally throughout his lifetime, and died exactly two months shy of his 100th birth-

day, actively attending to business and playing golf for his recreation. Birth date: July 8, 1839.

Field Marshal von Hindenburg had retired to his farm in
Pomerania, there to relax in rural tranquility and to enjoy the
companionship of his family and friends. But he was called
out of retirement at the age of 68. Yes, he had been a competent military leader in World War I, but certainly nobody
extraordinary. He reached international prominence between
the ages of 68 and 86, and made the pages of history in capi-
tals. (Birth: October 2, 1847.)

Those are males, we admit, the stronger sex, but look at
Grandma Moses, who was 100 years old on September 7,
1960. She was born in 1860.

But why go on? Look around your own circle of relatives
and friends and you will find many over 65 who are alert of
mind and agile and vigorous of body. Of course, they have to
take care of themselves physically, but don't we all?

If you have an active number vibration for your last life
cycle, a 5 or a 9, you are not likely to go into complete retirement. Some interests will keep you busy, being happy and
occupied, and at the same time will fill the larder with cash.

Look upon your second cycle as that of preparation along
economic lines, so you may enjoy an income during your
Harvest Cycle, regardless of the fact that you may keep on
being busy improving your financial status.

Negatively considered, the last cycle may also bring solitude, want, ill health and an enforced drudgery just to keep
the wolf from the door. That's why it would pay you to study
your cycle challenges. Try to forestall harassed conditions
for those dreaded "old age" years, when you're a burden to
others and nobody wants you. Such gloomy outlook is not
necessary, not when you live your life according to the dic-
tum of your numbers.

WHEN DO YOUR LIFE CYCLES CHANGE?

You've heard of the biblical three-score-and-ten span of
human existence. Divide it by three and you have approxi-
mately twenty-five years to each cycle.

But that is a very sketchy and rather superficial method of
calculating cycles. Numerology is exact and its rules are definite and precise, so you must understand that a special tech-

nique is required to figure out the exact beginning of your second or third cycles.

Let's say a young man has reached the age of 25, and that his life is changing from his Formative years to his Cycle of Productivity. He may want to make vocational changes, perhaps he is graduating from Law School or some other institute of learning. He wants to know and be sure where he stands in the cosmic pattern.

This depends upon his Personal Year number. Let's say he is in a "seven" year on his 25th birthday. That would mean he still has to go two more years before he reaches his next (middle) cycle. His cycle changed in his 27th year.

On the other hand, there is a young girl aged 25, who would like to get married at the right time according to her numberscope. She is in a "two" year, which would indicate that she had already turned the cycle period at the age of 23, and that she is now enjoying her second cycle. This "two" personal year would be ideal for her to promise to "love and obey."

You can readily see from this evaluation of the cyclic turn that it does *not* happen exactly at the age of 25, but around those years, when the transition is made from a 9 Personal Year to a *1* year. Remember, therefore, that the New Cycle begins always with a *1* Personal year.

The *1* to the *9* comprise the cycle of all human life periods and a new era in any personal existence cannot commence except in a *1* Personal Year.

Check back into your own past and figure out when the *1* Personal Year took place close to your 25th birthday. That year was the beginning of your Cycle of Productivity.

NUMBER VALUE OF YOUR CYCLE OF PRODUCTIVITY

(The Days of the Month)

Single digit numbers have a basic quality from *1* to *9*, but their variety is infinite. In this respect they can be likened to colors. Take blue, for instance. It is a root color, but innumerable shades from the light, heavenly blue to the deep violet and indigo tints come under the classification blue.

The same can be said of the units of measure in the mathematical system. There is a basic *1*, the first number of the scale. But when this *1* is the result of having been reduced from a number of several digits to a single digit, its intrinsic essence has been altered. It is no longer a simple *1*, plain and unadulterated, but it is a composite from other numbers. Applying this to the days of the month in relation to the Cycle of Productivity, a *1* cycle may have stemmed from a 10th, or 19th, or 28th birthday. It indicates an intensification of the fundamental *1*.

In the *19*, for instance, all numbers from the *1* to the *9* have been absorbed, therefore the *1* reduced from a *19* represents a higher octave than just a *1*. Always take into consideration when judging your cycle number that although you may belong to a *1* cycle, its essence will be more potent if it is derived from a *10*, or a *19*, or a *28*.

The *2* as a root number is the second one of the series. But there are many other "twos," composed of various number ingredients. This is the case when the *2* has been reduced from a 20th or 29th day of the month. This same principle applies to all single digit numbers. They are basic only as they represent the first nine numbers in the mathematical scale. If a *9* has been derived from adding a *1* to an *8*, as in the 18th birthday, it's not the plain *9* anymore, but vibrates on a higher octave.

Then where does the zero come into this scheme? When it crops up in a date like the 10th, 20th or 30th day of your birth month, it indicates a stepping-up of its numerical potency. When the *10* is reduced to a *1* by adding *1* to *0*, it belongs in the category of "ones" but nevertheless represents a higher octave than the basic *1*. The *20* is significant as an intensified *2*, and we associate the *30* with a super-personality, a stepping-up of the self-expression number *3*. If the *30* is your birthday vibration—if you were born on the 30th day of the month—you should not neglect some form of self-expression, either as a vocation or as a hobby. All cyclic numbers give you a definite vocational advice.

Then there are the so-called master numbers: *11* and *22*. These numbers can be reduced to a *2* in the case of the *11*, or to a *4* in the case of a *22* birthday. Such reduction to a basic single-digit number is usually justified, for only a few persons can fully exploit the hyper-potential challenge of these master numbers. Yet when a genius is born under the influence of a master number by virtue of his birthday either on the *11* or the *22*, extraordinary achievements could result. This is the case of Thomas Edison, born on February 11 and of Frederic Chopin, the composer, born February 22. Their achievement caliber amounted to sublime genius. The challenge of their master-number birthday was fully exploited by them.

Some numerologists will reduce a *29* birthday to an *11*, as in the case of Sigmund Romberg, born on the 29th day of July. Therefore, the *29* is often considered as belonging to the master numbers. Equally, they will not reduce the *22* if it is someone's birthday. Personally, we have found that if either the *11* or the *22* happens to be the birthday of a person not blessed by singular talents, their influences will result in confusion rather than in outstanding accomplishments. It would pay you to reduce these masternumbers to their single digits *2* or *4* if you happen to be engaged in an average, everyday occupation. That is, if these numbers apply to your middle cycle, that of Productivity.

Humanity as a whole dwells in the realm of averages and follows the line of least resistance in vocational matters. Let's face it, there are more jobs open to clerical workers ruled by the *4* than to composers ruled by the *22*. You may be happier and perhaps more successful if you function under the *2* as a repair man than under the *11* as an inventor. Take your choice occupationally and live up to the challenges of the simple single-digit numbers *2* or *4* or at the higher octave values of the *11* or the *22*.

Of course, the above advice applies to the Cycle of Productivity. Masternumbers, however, can also dominate your Harvest Cycle. Take the life of Arturo Toscanini, born in 1867, which reduces to a *22*. His career demonstrated that he obeyed his numerical challenge, for the *22* has affinity with musicianship. He proved an instrument of a superlative order in his interpretation of the symphonic music of the masters. The famous conductor lived and worked according to the pattern of a *22*. As an octogenarian he exploited the values of his birth year number, 1867, which ruled his last or Harvest Cycle.

By the same token, the *11* may also hold sway in one's Harvest Cycle. This was the case in the life of the ever-active and productive caustic wit, George Bernard Shaw, born in the year 1865, which adds up to an *11*. His electrifying sarcasm and his creative ability—not to forget his shrewd business acumen—were in evidence to the very last. Field Marshal von Hindenburg, though engaged in a military career, also demonstrated how a masternumber can rule one's destiny at the close of life. He was born in 1847, again an *11* challenge.

By the above analysis you can see that free-will is not denied any human being when directing one's life forces according to his or her number values. There are about 10,000 different vocations in this age of specialization you may choose from. Numbers do not tell you that you should be a plumber, or a schoolteacher, or an aviator. But they will acquaint you with your innate qualifications for a specific job. The practical unimaginative number values *4* or *8* do not encourage positions where mental ingenuity is required; introvert numbers such as the *7* fashion a bad salesman; and the restless *5* may prompt you to speculate and take vocational chances, but it acts as an obstacle to staid and stodgy clock-punching jobs.

Numbers represent a directive, they do not compel, for after all you are the ruler of your own destiny.

YOUR "ONE" MIDDLE CYCLE

(*Days of the Month: 1, 10, 19, 28*)

If you were born on the 1st, 10th, 19th or 28th day of any month, your Cycle of Productivity is marked by the number *1*. You should be endowed with an innate drive to achieve, for you long to do things better than the other fellow. Your sense of responsibility should be exemplary. Also you are imbued with boundless ambition to crash through to the top in any chosen field of endeavor. You strive to excel. Your sphere of activities may be limited, of course, but within your own circle you aspire to reach a prominent position. It follows logically that you are not cut out to play second fiddle.

A "1" Birthday

Map out a vocational route for yourself and follow it religiously. This should not be difficult, for your mental qualifications outshine those of your heart. You reason logically, and are practical withal. You have a great deal of perseverance and purposefulness to overcome obstacles. As a mental type you are not apt to be emotionally demonstrative, yet you crave affectional display from members of your immediate environment. Example: J. Edgar Hoover, FBI chief, born January 1st.

A "10" Birthday

This number is composed of a *1* plus *0* and represents an extension of the basic *1*. Perhaps that is why persons born on the 10th day of any month usually have more than one iron in the fire. Certainly you should have a vocation and an avocation. Your promotional ability and your creative vein are remarkable, therefore your number advises that you experiment with untried ventures. Example: Helen Hayes, actress, born October 10th.

A "19" Birthday

Composed of all the numbers from *1* to *9*, the 19 vibration of your Productivity Cycle is a fluctuating one. You forge ahead with dynamic enthusiasm, achieve a measure of success, then suddenly find yourself on the downward path. A zig-zag line describes your accomplishments. You may rise to a dizzying pinnacle and drop down to the bottom. But your amazing resourcefulness and speculative audacity come to your stead when you find yourself at the crossroads. You are quick to recuperate, both in cases of physical depletion or in moments of economic danger. You can take the count of *9*, get up and win the bout in the end. Example: Bernard Baruch, world economist, born August 19th.

A "28" Birthday

This number cycle is composed of the cooperative *2* and the practical, executive *8* and somehow represents the most affectional of all the *1* cycles. The lives of people so born are brimful with friendships and they are usually beloved by large groups of people, an excellent influence to project to the public. Your emotions are intense and feeling is usually the driving force behind your achievements. Your love of liberty is pronounced but you must be careful not to offend good taste by an unconventional behavior. Also do not lose interest in your endeavor and thereby become an ardent beginner and neglect to follow through on your victories. Example: Richard Rodgers, composer, born June 28th.

Persons of a *1* Cycle of Productivity are: Kate Smith, May 1st; Walter Reuther, September 1st; Fred Astaire, May 10th; Ray Bolger, January 10th; Clark Gable, February 1st; Guy

Lombardo, June 19; Prince Philip, June 10th; Helen Hayes, October 10th; Mary Martin, December 1st; Charles Boyer, August 28th; Hildegarde, February 1st; Prime Minister Harold Macmillan, February 10th; Clare Booth Luce, April 10th.

YOUR "TWO" MIDDLE CYCLE

(Days of the Month: 2, 11, 20, 29)

If you were born on the 2nd, 11th, 20th or 29th day of any month, your Cycle of Productivity is ruled by the 2. This is a gracious, friendly influence, which advises affable tactics, cooperation and persuasion. You succeed best in life if you keep an open mind and train yourself to see both sides of an issue. By attracting people to yourself you will also attract favorable conditions in business and career matters. Don't try to be a lone eagle but work with others. This is a "collector's" aspect. That means collect concrete information, stimulating friends and objects that are of interest to you. Combat sensitivity. Do not consider it beneath you to attend to little things, for the big opportunities will drop into your lap when least expected. Be pleasant under trying circumstances. Study. Be an inveterate reader. Knowledge is power to those born in a 2 cycle.

A "2" Birthday

Learn to function in a harmonious environment if you wish to succeed. Steer away from gloomy people. Nagging and fault-finding critics are bound to depress you. You can only do your best when you feel you are being appreciated by others. Have you a talent? Develop it by all means, if for no other purpose than to be a social asset in a gathering, or for your own enjoyment. Many creative artists, poets and writers, even outstanding celebrities, had a 2 Cycle of Productivity. Example: Bing Crosby, crooner, born May 2nd.

An "11" Birthday

This is a difficult number to operate under, for it requires constant self-discipline if you wish to fully exploit its hyperpotential influence. Try to steer by a level keel even under nervous duress. Keep emotions steady. This vibration tends to cause tremendous nervous tension, therefore many who are

ruled by the *11* are erratic and moody. The mentality is apt
to be brilliant above the average, but allow your intuitions to
function also. Don't rush toward extremes but travel the middle lane, if possible. Unusual vacations suit you to a T. Example: Long John Nebel, radio star, born June 11.

A "20" Birthday

An extension of the *2*, this number causes you to live in
the emotions and inclines you to crave companionship and
friends. In fact, you dislike the idea of living alone; hence
many of this cycle marry early in life, establish a well-ap-
pointed home and prefer to live in the country. It would be
wise for you to get a special occupational training and a thor-
ough education. A storehouse of practical knowledge will always come to your stead in vocational jobs. Attend to details
for which you seem to have a special knack. You may own a
business in association with others. A congenial, small-scale
business in which the major responsibility is assumed by others would suit you perfectly. Musical ability, love of arts, and
some special talent also are often in evidence. Example:
James Stewart, actor, May 20th.

A "29" Birthday

This number is frequently interpreted as an *11* when the *9*
and *2* are added, and is not reduced. It is then adjudged a
master-number. Therefore be not surprised that many an outstanding personality operated in this *29* cycle as an *11*. This
is an excellent aspect for a negotiator, for a moderator between opposing factions, for a diplomatic or political career.
Executives, inventors and artists also were born with a *29* for
middle cycle. But watch nerves! They may give your temper
the third degree and may make it difficult for others to work
with you. Banish depressed moods by absorbing interests and
a hard-driving occupation. Example: Dag Hammarskjöld,
Secretary-General of the UN, born July 29th.

Others with a *2* middle cycle are: Xavier Cugat, bandleader, January 2nd; President John F. Kennedy, May 29th;
Ingrid Bergman, actress, August 29th; Eleanor Roosevelt,
October 11th; Desi Arnaz, producer, March 2nd; Willie Har-
tack, jockey, December 11th; Sergei Rachmaninoff, composer, April 2nd; Mickey Mantle, baseball star, October 20th;

Dr. Joseph Rhine, psychologist, September 29th; Sigmund Romberg, composer, July 29th.

YOUR "THREE" MIDDLE CYCLE

(Days of the Month: 3, 12, 21, 30)

If you were born on the 3rd, 12th, 21st or 30th day of any month, you belong in a 3 middle cycle. This happens to be my own case, being born in December, a 3 month, and on the 30th day, also a 3 influence, and naturally I understand well how a 3 can influence a human life. Its challenge is precise and definite, for you are meant to bring cheer and joy into your surroundings, disperse gloom and bring light into darkness by virtue of a positive and encouraging personality. My vocation also is represented by this 3 number. As a bandleader I am constantly offering pleasant entertainment and am sought out to supply dance music at merry gatherings, at social functions, or teen-age prom affairs. If this is your middle cycle, do not neglect to fulfil your purpose in life: bring good cheer whenever possible.

A "3" Birthday

This is a challenge for self-expression, therefore you should engage in occupations where you can demonstrate an ability to write, and give your critical acumen a chance to be recognized. It's a busy number, and you should have several irons in the fire. "Keep moving!" should be your motto. You love people, are a good mixer, and function well before the public. There may be a touch of an exhibition complex in you, for you love to have an admiring audience. You are basically a restless type and need many interests to keep you busy. Your recuperative powers are excellent, for you bounce back quickly from any kind of physical depletion. Literature could be a vocation as well as an avocation. Example: Henry Luce, publisher, born April 3rd.

A "12" Birthday

It's not only what you know but whom you know if you wish to succeed in BIG letters with a 12 for your Cycle of Productivity. Seek places where you can make interesting and worthwhile contacts. There is a touch of genius about you, especially if you are the imaginative creative type. Your warm personality and friendly, convincing manner make you an excellent salesman, or promotional expert. Besides your practical mentality, you have usually some artistic talent which you should cultivate. But you have a drawback in your "down-in-the-boots" moments of discouragement and introversion. This is particularly the case when affections prove disappointing. Your love affairs and friendships play first fiddle in your life. The various branches of show business are suitable as vocations. Example: Oscar Hammerstein, lyricist, born July 12th.

A "21" Birthday

No better example for a *21* Cycle of Productivity than the charming personality and the fascinating life of Queen Elizabeth II of Great Britain, born April 21st. She has all the loveable attributes of a perfect *21*: a melodious speaking voice which she uses to advantage when making public addresses; a pleasing exterior, good taste in dress; and a magnetic manner of meeting high or low and winning their affection by her contagious smile. All *3* types have a tendency to brood, however, and are inclined to become depressed. But an occasion for cheer, such as an invitation to a dance or to attend an entertaining show, will cause you to snap out of your blues in no time. This is a self-expression number, and vocations are suitable where your interest in writing, publishing or editing could be exploited. Example: Ernest Hemingway, author, born July 21st.

A "30" Birthday

The world of show-business and the fourth estate are crowded with celebrities who have a *30* middle cycle. Somehow they could not help but drift into a realm of art, music, or literature, often against the disciplinarian barriers of parental opposition. You have the necessary dynamo and physical stamina to "take it," for a public life makes demands on your nervous system and your physical resistance. Fortunately you are immune, somehow, to contagious diseases and recuperate rapidly from any illness.

Try to accumulate as much concrete knowledge as possible, for you frequently lack the necessary information when arguing a point. You are intuitive and imaginative, and should guard against becoming confused when you plunge headlong into psychic experimentations.

There is no better companion in the number-scale than one of a *30* birthday for your sense of humor is refreshing. You make a loyal friend in spite of the fact that your flirtatious manner is often misleading. Example: Winston Churchill, British statesman, born November 30th.

Other persons born in *3* middle cycle are: Marlon Brando, actor, April 3rd; Fulton Lewis, radio commentator, May 30th; Vincent Lopez, band leader, December 30th; Deborah Kerr, actress, September 30th; Edward G. Robinson, actor, December 12th; Frank Sinatra, singer, December 12th; Lana Turner, actress, February 3rd; Prince Obolensky, hotelman, December 3rd.

YOUR "FOUR" MIDDLE CYCLE

(Days of the Month: 4, 13, 22, 31)

If you were born on the 4th, 13th, 22nd or 31st day of any month, you have a *4* middle cycle life pattern. Take courage in your destiny when you read the formidable list of all those famous personages who, like yourself, were saddled—so some numerologists contend—with a *4* Cycle of Productivity. Surely this is the Temple Four-Square of extraordinary achievements. It's a springboard to a successful life well lived. That is, if you exploit the *4* challenge of hard work, the powers of mental concentration and of dogged perseverance to forge ahead toward a definite goal. You are not readily sidetracked from any task, for your single-track mind helps you to stick by the guns even if the going is rough. Curb severity and harsh criticism of others. Cultivate tolerance.

A "4" Birthday

We point with pride toward a perfect bundle of joy, energy and spunk, namely the beloved singer-dancer-actress Doris Day, born April 4. Here is a life patterned after the *4*: a grim struggle to get parts, pressing domestic responsibilities and an economic pinch at the start of her career. All of this she overcame successfully and cheerfully to establish herself as a No. 1 box office attraction in show business. Charles Lindbergh, born February 4, is another example of a *4* middle cycle destiny who made good in a big way. And so can you—within the confines of your particular vocational set-up. You have substantial ideals: love of family, of home, of the stimulating relaxations of nature, and of your work. In fact, many 4 middle cycle types claim that their work or career is their vacation. But be warned to take time off to play and to take care of your health. You need a sabbatical occasionally like everyone else. Don't drive others as hard as you drive yourself. Be careful. Remember, "The smile wins!" Example: Francis Cardinal Spellman, born May 4th.

A "13" Birthday

Here is another maligned number, the supposedly evil *13*. And all because of ignorance in evaluating the high octave of this "Number of the Anointed" with its extraordinary possibilities. It is true that you frequently clash with your environment and have difficulty to demonstrate the warmth and affectionate nature which is deeply hidden in yourself. Learn to express your feelings, and you will suffer less from being misunderstood. This is an "earth" number, and you succeed best in real estate, with tangible assets, and if you are artistically inclined, you may have a talent for sculpture. An avocation of that sort sometimes becomes a profitable commercial asset in your economic budget. You are inclined to be un unimaginative and much of a disciplinarian, with the result that you could be an excellent manager. You have scientific and mechanical leanings. Example: Jack Straus, President, R. H. Macy Co., born January 13th.

A "22" Birthday

Reduce the 22 to a single digit and it becomes a plain *4*. In this case you should study what has been said of the *4* as a middle cycle number and apply it to your particular needs. But if you are able to meet the high-frequency of the *22* influence, you should try to expand your consciousness to wider mental and spiritual horizons. It is a master-number, and indicates a departure from the average mode of human existence. Many adventuresome experiences may be met by you, even weird clashes with psychic phenomena. Then keep your mental balance and keep your feet on the ground. Your mission in life is to help humanitarian causes, to work for the public good rather than for selfish ulterior motives and personal aggrandizement. Example: General Charles DeGaulle, President of France, born November 22nd.

A "31" Birthday

This number *31* is a reversed *13*, and again we hear a lot of negative criticism that is a difficult influence to work with as a middle cycle. It is true that such lives are often beset by bitter disappointments on the material plane, and frustrations are plentiful in the love life. Therefore, we again advise that you cultivate the influence of the simple *4* and apply its advice to your affairs. That means: Have an all-consuming interest, apply yourself wholeheartedly to a task, even to a hobby, learn to express your feelings and affections, cultivate worthwhile friends, and, above all, pay attention to health. You also should learn to handle money wisely and avoid financial losses due to foolish investments or trusting in advisers who are unscrupulous. Example: Tallulah Bankhead, actress, born January 31st.

Other persons born with a *4* middle cycle are: Maria Callas, opera star, December 4th; Joe Louis, prize fighter, May 13th; William Saroyan, playwright, August 31st; Louis Armstrong, band leader, July 4th; Rainier, Prince of Monaco, May 31st; Mike Todd, producer, July 22nd; Mitzi Gaynor, September 4th; Charlton Heston, actor, October 4th; Chiang Kai-shek, October 31st; Kim Novak, actress, February 13th; Drew Pearson, columnist, December 13th; Sophie Tucker, entertainer, January 13th.

YOUR "FIVE" MIDDLE CYCLE

(Day of the Month: 5, 14, 23)

If you were born on the 5th, 14th or 23rd day of any month, you belong in the category of those with a *5* Cycle of Productivity. This is a pivotal influence, subject to sudden turning-points, to changes of mental attitudes and switches of your affectional objects. That's why you must learn never to plan too far ahead. Make no rigid appointments, for you may not be able to keep them. You cannot be blamed for such reversals of conduct or changes of plans. It's your destiny and the vibration of the *5* that account for your inability to follow a rigid itinerary. By the same token, vocational positions that call for humdrum clock-punching will not prove successful for you. Follow the line of least resistance and live from day to day. Change your plans like a captain in battle, and you will succeed amazingly and in an undreamt-of, unexpected manner.

A "5" Birthday

Versatility is your middle name, vocationally considered, hence select an occupation where you find originality and ingenuity come into play. Shift of scene also is favored, as for instance in travelling jobs, with steamship companies, and travel agencies. Your mind moves rapidly. You can adjust quickly to almost any kind of emergency, hence you make good as a salesman, as a promoter, and do well in the brokerage business. You're better suited for the outer office than for desk executive positions. Excellent for contact making, for reconnoitering new business projects, for advertising and public relations activities. You love to run the gamut of human experiences and to drink freely from the cup of romance. You may have a singing voice, or musical ability. But creativity along artistic lines is your long suit even as a hobby. Example: Walt Disney, cartoonist, born December 5th.

A "14" Birthday

Being composed of a *1* plus *4* makes the number *14* a potential level for expansion in business or career matters. You cannot help but drift toward public recognition, even in a minor way, even as a sort of local hero. This is a "dual number," for you are both creative and critical at the same time. Your middle cycle is usually marked by some drastic adjustment which comes upon you like a bolt from the blue. It is almost like a complete switch from red to blue, or vice-versa. Take as an example the career of Dwight D. Eisenhower, born October 14th, a military man upon whom greatness was thrust when he became President of the United States. Or even his wife Mamie, born November 14th, who graduated from simple housewife to First Lady of the Land. Women of this *4* cycle should marry young. Avoid the temptations of the flesh—drink, gambling and flirtatious indulgences. You can best be appealed to by your emotions. You often think as you feel. A public career is a good bet vocation-wise. Example: Jack Benny, comedian, February 14th.

A "23" Birthday

You have an almost mysterious knack of diagnosing physical ailments, or faulty economic conditions that hamper the smooth path of progress in vocational, or career matters, or in business ventures. Hence you could be a healer of the physical body, or a trouble-shooter in business ventures that seem to get nowhere. You belong to the performing arts rather than the creative arts, a reason why many actors and actresses have a 23 for their middle cycle number. But you do excel also in practical business organizations as a promoter, salesman and advertiser. You are fond of socializing with congenial friends and make new acquaintances readily. You try to get the best out of life, are completely void of a martyr complex, but push ahead unabashed when conquering new worlds in business and profession. Example: Shirley Temple, actress and TV performer, born April 23rd. Others with a 5 middle cycle: Gene Kelly, dancer, August 23rd; Walter Pidgeon, September 23rd; Adlai Stevenson, politician, February 5th; Joan Crawford, actress, March 23rd; J. Arthur Rank, producer, December 23rd; Dr. Wernher von Braun, rocket expert, March 23rd; Bette Davis, April 5th.

YOUR "SIX" MIDDLE CYCLE

(Days of the Month: 6, 15, 24)

If you were born on the 6th, 15th or 24th day of any month, your Middle Cycle is ruled by the 6, the number of adjustments. This means that you should deal with people and their problems, from members of the intimate circle of your home and family to the greater needs of humanity. However, you are an idealist and look for perfection, which is rarely realized in life. This causes you often to feel frustrated with your mission in life. You love beauty and harmony in your surroundings and could make a fine interior decorator. But your greatest vocational calling is in the theatre. Nearly all persons ruled by a 6 middle cycle possess the gift of mimicry in a large degree.

A "6" Birthday

Praise and appreciation for your abilities are a driving force in your vocational aspirations. And affection and love are an even greater need for your happiness in private life. Being an emotional type fashions you for an artistic career and for literary pursuits rather than for mechanics or abstract sciences. A business job also could offer opportunities. You could head your own venture preferably in association with others. Whatever it is you select for yourself as your life job, don't go it alone. You excel in teamwork, collaboration, working with groups in congenial surroundings. Family or friends often play a prominent part in your career selection. Example: Milton Eisenhower, born September 15th.

A "15" Birthday

This number presents an interesting contradiction: while you are cooperative, even submissive, to loved ones and those you work with in a position, you still resent domination. No one can lord it over you. You would chafe under harsh, domineering treatment by a supervisor or a member of your family to a degree where you would actually be ailing. Quit a job where you feel uncomfortable and out of place with co-workers. Your vocational qualifications run along professional lines, rather than in the commercial field. If your academic education has equipped you with special learning, you should make a fine diplomat, lawyer, lecturer or teacher. You could also make a good physician but have not the innate gift for surgery. The sight of blood would offend your artistic sensibility. A home environment is necessary for your health, which is generally satisfactory. Your musical or artistic leanings are more pronounced than your scientific talents.

A "24" Birthday

If this dual number is your birthdate, you are an active, restless type and should keep on being busy right along. Retirement is not for you even in your Harvest Cycle. You seem to have boundless energy that craves doing something, and you will feel like exploding if this sense of activity is pent up in wasted time. You have several avenues to occupational success open for you: the arts, stage and music might call you strongly, for you may be imbued with various talents. But you could also succeed as a promoter, banker or financier. A profession is suitable for you rather than a job in a drab, colorless business atmosphere. Example: Thomas Dewey, politician, born March 24th.

Other persons with a 6 Cycle of Productivity: Elsa Maxwell, May 24th; Lowell Thomas, April 6th; Jack Dempsey, boxer, June 24th; Lucille Ball, actress, August 6th; Babe Ruth, baseball star, February 6th; Ethel Barrymore, August 15th; Lilli Palmer, actress, May 24th.

YOUR "SEVEN" MIDDLE CYCLE

(Days of the Month: 7, 16, 25)

If you were born on the 7th, 16th or 25th day of any month, your Cycle of Productivity is ruled by the number 7. This influence has often been called a sacred ray, for no other number carries with it a stronger element of destiny than this particular one. Things will be attracted to you, they will come *to* you. But no matter how you strive and struggle, there is no accomplishment shown unless the cosmos is ready for it. That's why mental analysis is more important than high-pressure action. Reflection and meditation win out over aggressive initiative. Also, you must appreciate the fact that solitude means replenishing your worn nerve batteries that have been depleted in the struggle with grim reality. Be not afraid of aloneness with yourself. Live in a world of ideas and ideals. Work on fundamentals; aspire for higher spiritual levels; be a philosopher and alone. That means, avoid binding partnerships unless they are consummated on spiritual levels.

A "7" Birthday

Learn to project specialized accomplishments and let your achievements get publicity or recognition for you. Follow the voice of your intuitions, of your keen inventive genius and the better advice that stems from the "small still voice within." If you have a talent for creativity—musical, literary or artistic—develop it, and produce the best you can. Slipshod efforts and mediocre products just don't belong in a 7 cycle. Projection of art through mechanical means is also favored, such as motion pictures, radio, TV, or recording efforts. The realm of show business is ruled by the 7. In chemistry, research, laboratory work, what could be more inspirational than a 7 stimulation, just to mention for our example a world-famous physicist: Madame Marie Curie, discoverer of radium, born November 7th.

A "16" Birthday

When you hear the name of Mary Baker Eddy, born on

July 16th, you just *know* that this number turns the mind toward spiritual verities. There is an element of aloofness from worldly aspects and the need to commune with the invisible realm proves both inspirational and profitable. Do not neglect your metaphysical urges to investigate the secret laws of nature. Such information could prove helpful in developing your intrinsic abilities for literature, poetry or musicianship. On the material or economical plane you would do well as a broker, banker, or TV or radio moderator. With all such inspirational talents you also could be endowed with a keen reasoning and analytical acumen for a practical business career.

Philosophy is a greater spiritual uplift for you than dogmatic religions. Unusual vocations are suitable. Example: Barbara Stanwyck, born July 16th.

A "25" Birthday

This number is composed of a *2*, the vibration of cooperation, and a *5*, the influence for creativity and salesmanship, hence no better number for outstanding successes along almost any avenue of endeavor. Great producers of the theatre (David Belasco, July 25), inventors along mechanical lines and discoverers of nature's secret phenomena (Marconi, April 25) and titans of philosophy (Ralph Waldo Emerson, May 25) all were born with this number *25* for their Cycle of Productivity. If this is your birthday, you are not a surface personality but are able to conceal your innermost thoughts and feelings. You may abound with talent, and if you develop some line of self-expression you should surely be successful in commercializing it. Try to become interested in the lofty, constructive side of politics. Garner global information, and see how other nations operate. The State Department could offer splendid opportunities for your talents. Example: John Foster Dulles, born February 25th.

Others with a *7* Middle Cycle are: Charlie Chaplin, April 16th; Robert Ripley, December 25th; Cab Calloway, band leader, December 25th; Leonard Bernstein, conductor, August 25th; Edgar Bergen, ventriloquist, February 16th; Grandma Moses, artist, September 7th; Joe DiMaggio, November 25th.

YOUR "EIGHT" MIDDLE CYCLE

(Days of the Month: 8, 17, 26)

If you were born on the 8th, 17th or 26th day of any month, your Cycle of Productivity is ruled by the power number 8. It's of an earth element and synchronizes to material possessions. That means accumulation of wealth—tangible assets, or cash! You of such a Middle Cycle should meet up with innumerable fine opportunities for aggrandizement along economic lines. These should be fully exploited by you. Therefore, be alerted to their manifestation in your destiny and make the most of it. You can miss out also for lack of being aware of their presence. As Ralph Waldo Emerson once said, "He is a wise man who recognizes his opportunity when it comes." The 8 consciousness inspires efficiency in matters of economic solidity if not actually in accumulating excess wealth.

An "8" Birthday

Financial mastery is your challenge if this influence of the practical 8 represents your Middle Cycle. You should be active in a world of practical values. Operate against a commercial or financial background. This is the perfect business number and an economic set-up should offer vocational possibilities for you. Try to achieve prominence, perhaps power, through wise handling of monetary assets and investments. Women of this cycle often marry for money. They feel marriage offers economic security, and that a husband should be a good provider and breadwinner. However, if the marriage vessel goes on the rocks of failure, these fine mates step forward to meet the call of vocational assistance. All you of this cycle, men or women, should use your money consciousness to reach complete economic independence in order to enjoy freedom in your last cycle, that of Harvests. Example: John D. Rockefeller, Sr., oil magnate, born July 8th. Sharing this birth date, though not the birth year, is his grandson, Nelson Rockefeller, Governor of New York, also born July 8th.

A "17" Birthday

A perfect influence for a banker, broker, agent or financier if it happens to be your birthday. All executives, directors or lawyers, as well as corporation officers, high or low, can consider themselves blessed with this money consciousness. You could also be at the head of your own business, or enjoy a partnership in a large corporation. However, since this number is composed of a *1* and a *7*, you should protest against interference in your handling of affairs. Also you would do wise to let underlings attend to the details which often annoy you. Your forte is mapping out the big campaigns on the battlefield of commerce and finance. It may not surprise you to learn that the New York Stock Exchange was born on a *17* birthday, namely May 17th, 1792. Besides the world of finance, the government and administration of organized groups, such as hospitals, schools, etc., also offer suitable positions for you. Example: Gaylord Hauser, nutritionist, born May 17th.

A "26" Birthday

Quite a change in this number from either the simple *8* or the composite *17*, for now we find cooperation and congenial associations to beckon for you born under this vibration. Whatever field you select depends upon your innate talents and occupational equipment. It could be in the field of art and literature, even in the theatre and motion picture world. But you could also automatically gravitate toward power and money that beckon in a business enterprise. You are able to commercialize your talents in a big way, no matter what your selection of a vocation might be. Politics, government, administrative positions in corporate organizations certainly promise success for you if "efficiency" in your work is your password. Always try to maintain a level degree of interest in what you are doing. For when your ambition and ability are harmoniously balanced you could reach prominence in any chosen field of endeavor until ripe old age. Example: George Bernard Shaw, playwright, born July 26th.

Other famous persons with an *8* Middle Cycle are: Sonja Henie, skating star, April 8th; Ex-President Harry S. Truman, May 8th; John Wayne, actor, producer, director, May 26th; Emile Coué, psychotherapist, February 26th; Elvis Presley, singer, January 8th; Emlyn Williams, playwright, November 26th; Betty Hutton, TV star, February 26th.

A "NINE" MIDDLE CYCLE

(Days of the Month: 9, 18, 27)

If you were born on the 9th, 18th or 27th day of any month your Middle Cycle is ruled by the *9*. Here is an influence which belongs in the category of universal numbers, introducing a global outlook on business affairs and in vocational matters. "Expand your viewpoints and widen your mental horizons," should be your challenge. This could be from a spiritual angle, for you may feel the call for some humanitarian activities. But you may reach for public recognition as well in some other line of work, artistic, literary, or in the ordinary walks of life against a business background. The 9, however, is somewhat tricky and misleading in that not everyone with such Middle Cycle is able to exploit it properly. The danger is always present that you may overreach your innate possibilities. But if you are cognizant of your limitations and try not to reach for the moon, ultimate success and prestige within your circle of vocational endeavor should be yours. The 9, as you have previously been taught, is a number of culmination. This offers another warning: Do not start too many *new* things or enterprises in this cycle. You may not be able to finish them and they may flounder on the rocks of failure. Bringing ventures already started to culmination should be your challenge after due changes and adjustments have been made. The 9, being a global influence, often introduces the occasion for long journeys and visits to foreign lands. Additionally, you may discover that you have a gift of being a versatile linguist. Interest in strange lands and foreign nations and their peoples and customs is frequently an innate part of your consciousness. Example: President Richard M. Nixon, born January 9th.

An "18" Birthday

Here is a real challenge—a number composed of the leadership value *1* and the economic, business number *8*. It is a strong pointer that your vocational pattern shows many facets which could be manifest in a variety of interests. The *8* advises practical lines, gigantic movements, political or economical, and business or strictly financial opportunities. The main advice comes from the *1*, however, to be at the helm no matter how large the enterprise may be. You should be qualified for efficient handling of details when running an organization. The world of legislature also should be suitable for some vocational expression, from judge to corporation lawyer. You reason logically and are good at debate. Hence public speaking, newspaper jobs, journalism, all should prove congenial as an occupational outlet. Your fine sense of efficiency makes you careful in matters of monetary spending. Example: Robert Moses, director of the 1964 World Fair, born December 18th.

A "27" Birthday

This 9, which stems from a composition of 2 and 7, presents an influence which makes you less self-sufficient or self-centered than the other two 9's of this Middle Cycle. In fact, it is more promising than the others for happy companionship, friendships and even a marriage that could endure. Of course, you too would want to function at the top of large organizations, or be at the helm of your own business. But there is this reservation: Have no partner who is on the same level as yourself. Associate only with those somewhat beneath you in the structure of an organization. A 50-50 partnership is not likely to prove successful. Money matters arouse your greatest sense of responsibility, for which reason you could be entrusted with managing the estates of others, as a custodian. Practice tolerance and patience. If things go wrong, you are apt to display resentment, even baffling introverted moods. Your religious convictions are pronounced, probably because of the "God-conscious" influence of the 7. Many of this number 27, no matter in what walk of life they wander, drift toward public recognition. Example: Leo Durocher, baseball manager, born July 27th.

Other famous folk born under this numerical influence for their Middle Cycle are: Bertrand Russell, philosopher, born May 18th; Ed Wynn, comedian, November 9th; Greta Garbo, actress, September 18th; Lucius Beebe, globe-trotter, December 9th; Cary Grant, actor, January 18th; Clarence Birdseye, frozen food expert, December 9th; Perry Como, TV artist, May 18th.

The Productivity Cycle numbers discussed above are interpreted according to their pure essence as they represent the vibrations of the days of the month from 1 to 31. But it must be understood that their respective numerical values are modified by the Path of Destiny numbers.

A person with a "nineteen" Middle Cycle in an "eight" Life pattern should function at the helm of an organization, while this very same "nineteen" influence would be made more potent by a parallel "one" Path of Destiny. Such a person should operate as a lone eagle in any given sphere of activity.

Always combine the numerical values of the Middle Cycle with that of the Life Path when analyzing a numberscope.

III

Your Name

THERE IS A CURIOUS conviction held by many numerologists that the unborn ego, if given a name before birth by his natural parents, will see the light at a time when the cosmic pattern is in harmony with that name.

Let's say Mr. and Mrs. Brown cherish the hope that their next offspring be a girl. They are planning on a girl and are naming her after her two grandmothers, Mary and Winifred. Obviously, this child, by her birth, continues the cosmic rhythm of life by perpetuating the existence on earth of two people, man and woman, through whom her birth is made possible. No one else is qualified cosmically to give the unborn ego a name, only her parents, whose life cycle she continues. This name had been bestowed upon the unborn ego before birth: that is important!

The wishes of the parents are fulfilled. Little Mary Winifred Brown is born, miraculously according to the pattern of numbers. For it happened on a day when her Path of Destiny and her baptismal name were in complete harmony according to Numerology.

But suppose the Browns are disappointed and instead of Mary Winifred they have a son whom they did not expect and for whom they have not selected a name. The boy is born nameless, and, helter-skelter, a name is chosen for him, according to regulations of the Department of Health, and registered there, within three days after birth. The parents named him Walter Travis Brown, and this name is tagged on the boy for life from the cradle to the grave. Walter Travis never liked his name. He thought it wasn't "lucky"; perhaps it was not harmonious with the concord of his Destiny.

This points up the fact that our baptismal name given us by our natural parents is an important factor in the scheme of our lives. It reveals certain character traits and its number total should harmonize with either the numerological value of our Path of Destiny, or the vibrations of our Cycle of Productivity.

How can a name be numerically analyzed, you may wonder. This is a very simple matter which anyone can master in no time. Each letter of the alphabet has its own numerical value, beginning with the A, which vibrates to *1*, and ending with the Z, with a number value of *8*. It is very easy for you to find the number for any letter in your name by consulting the following Letter-Number graph:

$$1—2—3—4—5—6—7—8—9$$

A	B	C	D	E	F	G	H	I
J	K	L	M	N	O	P	Q	R
S	T	U	V	W	X	Y	Z	

You see from the above that the number scale from *1* to *9* comes into consideration, but that the master-numbers *11* and *12* are omitted. Still, many numerologists assign to the letter V the master-number *22* and to K the *11*. However, these master-numbers may turn up in the total of name letters when the name is analyzed for its numerical pattern.

When a name is mathematically broken down, the vowels are separately evaluated from the consonants. See for yourself: the vowels have the following numbers:

A—*1*
E—*5*
I—*9*
O—*6*
U—*3*
Y—*7*

The dual letter Y can be either a vowel or a consonant.

Take the word *Y*esteryear. Each Y here is a consonant, but still maintains its vibration 7.

But in the words Dorothy or Henry the Y is a vowel, by virtue of its positional value in a word, as it *follows* a consonant.

When you break down a name for its letter value by numbers, watch for the Y. Count it among the vowels when at the end of a word and when the tonal accent rests upon it. But when at the beginning of a word or of a syllable it becomes a consonant.

HOW TO CALCULATE THE
NUMBER VALUES OF NAMES

Write a full name on a line allowing enough space at the top and at the bottom where you can place the respective numbers for either the vowels or the consonants.

The numbers of the vowels are placed *above* the name.

The numbers of the consonants are placed *below* the name.

Add up the total of the vowel numbers, and reduce to a single digit. Add up the total of the consonant numbers and reduce to a single digit.

The vowel number signifies the Ideality or Soul, representing the inner man or woman.

The consonant number signifies the Impression, for this projects the outer man, the qualities most easily detected by his fellow-beings.

The sum-total of the vowel number and the consonant number is called the Expression.

We give you herewith some examples of how to analyze a complete baptismal name, given at birth by his parents and registered in Department of Health.

Our first example is that of a world-famous animated cartoon artist and film producer, whose cornerstone letter synchronizes with his Cycle of Productivity.

Walt Disney, Born December 5, 1901

```
     1       9  5 7              total: 4 )
W A L T   D I S N E Y                     ) total: 6
   5  3 2   4   1 5              total: 2 )
    10            10
```

The Soul Urge of Walt Disney's name is *4;* his Impression number digits to *2;* and his Expression totals to *6.*

Every item in the name analysis of this great artist is important.

The *4* as a Soul Urge reflects correctly the nature of his work, that is the "animation" of his cartoons. You will recall that the *4* has affinity with technology, and what could be more representative than animated cartoons of the artist's *4* Soul Urge?

Walt Disney was the head of a tremendous organization, calling for the adjustment number *6*, represented in his total name. Without the ability to adjust to all types of personnel in his vast production realm, Walt Disney could not have created his masterpieces.

Also of importance is his Cornerstone letter, the W of Walt, which vibrates to *5*. This is the number of influence of his Middle Cycle, called the Cycle of Productivity: December *5*.

Another example is that of a beloved woman, Mary Baker Eddy, founder of Christian Science and author of the book *Science and Health*. Here you find a complete harmony to exist between the sum-total of the numerical value of the vowels in her name, ruled by the *8*, and her Path of Destiny number, also ruled by the *8*, the number of organization.

Mary Baker, Born July 16, 1821

Her birthday analysis presents no difficulties. Her birth month is July—*7*; her birthday is a *16*, reduce to *7*; and her birth year is 1821, reduce to *3*. Add: 7+7+3, the result is *8*. This is the number of her Path of Life: *8*.

It is amazing how her name vibrations—both of the vowels and the consonants in her name—correlate to the numbers in her birthdate.

$$\begin{array}{ccc} 8 & 6 & 3 \\ \overline{\text{M A R Y}} & \overline{\text{B A K E R}} & \overline{\text{E D D Y}} \\ 4 & 4 & 8 \end{array} \quad \begin{array}{l} \text{total: } 8 \\ \text{total: } 7 \end{array} \Big\} \quad \text{total: } \underline{15\text{--}6}$$

The vowels in Mary Baker Eddy's name reduce to an *8*. The vowels represent the soul, and in her case, its numerical value equals that of her Path of Destiny: *8*.

However, the sum-total of the consonants in her name, which picture the obvious traits and aims of the ego, are ruled by a *7*. This is the God-inspired number, the vibration of the priest and philosopher. Mary Baker Eddy was known to all—to her followers and ultimately to the world—as the founder of Christian Science. This *7* appears in her birthdate,

in her month and day vibrations. The total of her name is
pictured by the *6*, the number of love and humanitarianism,
harmonious with *8*.

Here is the name of a man familiar to all the world and
bound to be in the public eye for many years to come.

John Fitzgerald Kennedy, born May 29th, 1917

His birthdate digits to the following month: May (*5*);
birthday: 29, or *11*; birthyear 1917, or *9*. His formative cycle
was represented by the *5*, and it suggests according to his life
pattern that there were many trips and voyages for him. He
even attended college in England.

His Middle Cycle of Productivity was signified by the master-number *11*. This pictured his political career.

The *9* symbolized his last life cycle, or Harvest period in
his destiny. As we know, one of his great assets was his ability to project his personality, nationally and internationally.

His name can be broken down to the following numberscope.

VOWELS

6	9	5 1	5	5 7

J O H N   F I T Z G E R A L D   K E N N E D Y

Total: *38*, or *11*

CONSONANTS

J O H N   F I T Z G E R A L D   K E N N E D Y

1	8 5 6	2 8 7	9	3 4 2	5 5	4

Total: *69*, reduce to *15*, or *6*.

Add vowels and consonants together:
Vowels: *11;* consonants: *6;* total: *8*
John F. Kennedy had a master number in his name, an *11;*
it represented the vowel total, symbolizing his Soul Urge, also
called the Ideality. This is most significant, inasmuch as the
President had an *11* for his Cycle of Productivity influence,
synchronizing with his soul vibration.

The consonants total to *6*, the aspect of charm and affability which secured for him lasting popularity. This is called

the "Impression number," for it stands for all the traits that are most obvious to any casual observer.

The total of the vowel and consonant numbers add to *8*, the vibration of power through material possessions. This name total is called the "Expression" in number terminology.

IDEALITY—IMPRESSION—EXPRESSION

IDEALITY: The vowels in your name reveal the vibration of your Soul Urge, also called your Ideality. It is represented here by the *11*, but remember that K in a name is also counted as an *11*. So that this master-number *11* is strongly expressed in the name of J.F.K.

This *11* urge is basically of the "air" or mental element, which accounted for Jack Kennedy's literary leanings and his obvious intellectualism. The idealism of his soul was paramount, this expressed itself in an ideal toward humanity, but also in his belief in God. There is a tragic twist here in that he was concerned with humanity and universalism but frequently lacked psychological insight into the individuals he contacted. This caused some enmity. Abstractism is another virtue which, when overdone, may boomerang, for the simple reason that he may have been concerned with the welfare of mankind as an ideal and be blind to the immediate needs of those in his environment. Impulsiveness is frequently the cause for such oversight of the feelings of others. The *11* has sometimes been called the "Christ number" because the devotional ardor to a spiritual ideal is great. There could have been a touch of the martyr complex in his Soul Urge.

IMPRESSION of one's name is revealed by the consonants; in the case of our example it is the *6*. This is a very personal expression, for the family members played a great part not only in his emotional development and character formation; but they also played—as in this case—a vital part in his career progress. Of course he loved his home; wife and children are an inspiration and furnished his needed relaxation and companionship. The pleasures of the fireside were much in evidence, and *7* of his Path of Destiny is an obvious indicator that the way to his happiness led to a rural environment. He was not above admiring flowers and the landscape beauty surrounding a perfectly ordered household.

But the outstanding virtue of this number *6* for a President of the prestige of Mr. Kennedy was his knack of securing general popularity for himself.

EXPRESSION: After figuring the total letter numbers of the vowels and consonants separately, we naturally add them together. The result is the powerful *8* in Mr. Kennedy's name. This is the vibration of the executive, or shall we say the Chief Executive in his case, the builder of vast empires, the consultant and promoter of big ideas. He could also have been a connoisseur of art objects and an organizer of philanthropic activities. At any rate, he could function as the Head of State, with grace and dignity.

When summing up all these letter numbers we meet up with the "perfect three" the Greeks extolled in their numerical system. In our Table we find first the vowels, called the Soul Urge, which is that mysterious Great Within; then the consonants with their pointer at our obvious characteristics, which is the Great Without. Finally we contemplate the total man or woman, the personality that really matters in this struggle for existence and in our striving for higher levels in evolution.

Always look for some numerical tie-up between the letters in a name and the Soul Urge vibration and the identical number aspects in his or her birth date.

In our example we found the *11* to predominate in the Soul Urge of Mr. Kennedy and the letter K (*11*) of his surname to synchronize with the *29* of his Productivity Cycle. In my own case (born December 30th) the *3* is paramount, and correlates with the key-letter L (*3*) of Lopez. Now digit the word "band": *2+1+5+4.* There you have it, another *3.* Perhaps this accounts for the fact that I steered toward bandleading as a career when still in my Formative Cycle (December 3) or in ordinary language, when still in my teens.

Numbers are useful when applied to daily life. They are a pointer at our directives when making far-reaching decisions. Let's take the case of President Richard Milhous Nixon, born January 9, 1913. The universal *9*, which is the vibration of culmination and completion, dominates his Middle Cycle. On November 8, 1960, that eventful Election Day, Mr. Nixon lived through a *9* Personal Day, and was facing a *9* year in 1961. Would this not mean an "ending" of one kind of life period for him, rather than the beginning of a new career cycle as the Chief Executive in the White House? Count on a *9* in your destiny pattern as a finish of one thing followed by a turning point in a different direction.

Numbers may indicate what's generally called "good fortune." But do you always know what's good for you? One's destiny pattern can rarely be outwitted by the human mind, which accounts for the fact that both numbers and astrological interpretations may spring surprises on a person.

THE MAGIC SQUARE

There are innumerable Magic Squares in existence. The earliest ones date back to the days of Pythagoras, the father of arithmetic (6th Century B.C.). His square was based on the trinity for the Greeks favored the *3*. He also included the master-numbers *11* and *22* in his geometrical figure.

The Arabs based their square on the *10,* that is, 10×10, for they were the originators of the decimal system. And during the Middle Ages when the Inquisition held sway and Hermetic Societies protected the findings of numerology and astrology, the Magic Square formats were guarded carefully, and thereby handed down to posterity.

The accompanying Magic Square is based on the *3,* that is the 3×3 format, and is used in the Western system of Numerology (also called the Pythagorean System).

It is helpful and rather important when analyzing a name as to its vibratory potency. Are there any missing numbers in your name? Or perhaps you have an accumulation of certain letters which would emphasize outstanding phases of your destiny? A preponderance of a letter number as well as the complete absence of it indicate not only your character traits but also peculiar event-features in your life. For your existence here on earth runs in harmony with the cosmic rhythm, and nothing can happen, or does happen that is not in conformity with these universal laws. And that is what numbers indicate: the law of periodicity and rhythm.

In order to analyze your name accurately, and that of your friends, or family members, we urge you to study the Magic Square system of checking on the letters in any given name. See what's missing, for missing numbers are a pointer toward the challenges that the ego must meet in this life.

HOW IT IS DONE

1.	2.	3.
4.	5.	6.
7.	8.	9.

Read the rows from left to right.

No. 1 or top row, signifies: Your personal self: 1, 2, 3.

No. 2 or middle row, signifies: Your social numbers, namely the 4, 5, 6.

No. 3 or bottom row, signifies the universal trine, the numbers 7, 8, 9.

The master numbers *11* and *22* are reduced to a *2* and *4* respectively.

Applying this Magic Square technique to the name of John Fitzgerald Kennedy, we find that he had all numbers represented. He had no missing numbers.

Please place each respective number of his name into the sector where it belongs. The *1* goes into the upper left hand square. He had two numbers *1* in his name, and only one *3*.

The *5* goes into the center square. It is logical, for this number is pivotal, and all others gyrate around it. It is like the hub of a wheel with the spokes leading outward toward the rim. In our example we find six *5*'s, the number which is predominating in this figure.

Continue in this fashion through all the various letter numbers of his name. Insert each number in its proper sector, and check on the total. You will discover that the number *3* is the least represented in this figure and that the *5* is by far in the majority.

NAME-SCOPE OF JOHN FITZGERALD KENNEDY

One: 2	Two: 2	Three: 1
Four: 2	Five: 6	Six: 2
Seven 2	Eight: 2	Nine: 2

With no numbers missing there is just one interpretive con-culsion to draw: John Fitzgerald Kennedy had things handed to him on a silver salver. He had all the advantages of a care-ful rearing, loving parents who looked after a topnotch aca-demic training and fed his affectional needs. His "soulhood" was given opportunity to develop without impediment—he grew like a tree in the meadow. His vocational aspirations, represented by the action-hungry 5, were eagerly encouraged by both parents. The 9 being represented twice shows the ed-ucational opportunities offered him when travelling abroad, and when studying the customs and ways in foreign lands. He went to college in England to widen his mental horizons. Marriage beckoned with a charming girl of wealth and social prestige. Is there anything amiss in this protected, privileged existence?

Oh yes, there is! Look at all those many 5's he had to con-quer, pointing toward inner restlessness, to the danger of fall-ing victim to pressures when opinions are formed, the high tension of the nervous system. These drawbacks are not ob-vious in the "outer" life, but churned and swirled like a tur-bine in his breast, and their uneven, eddying motions were bound to buffet his soul about to extremes, from one erratic viewpoint to another.

The numerical high-frequency in Mr. Kennedy's number-scope is quite apparent. The prominent 11 needs a solid 4 to stabilize it. Instead there is an overdose of 5's to even fur-ther stimulate the hyper-potential vibratory rate of his destiny pattern.

His challenge was by no means a missing number, but the "too-muchness" of a good thing, the 11 and the 5.

Too many 5's in a name indicate an adventuresome spirit

and a hunger for constant changes. The desire to roam the Seven Seas of the globe amounts to compulsion. Such personalities tire quickly of any specific interest and are perpetually in quest for new worlds to conquer. Patience is lacking; tolerance should be cultivated; that virtue, loyalty to peoples and to causes, is a frequent void. Add to this the nervous tension of the *11* high-frequency, which is idealistic, to be true, but in many cases impractical.

The advantage of this letter-number combine is a striving for newness in production, to get away from the beaten path. We should expect a departure from old concepts and this, perhaps, was the cosmic manifestation about to be fulfilled by this Man of Destiny, who warrants a carefully-detailed number analysis in these pages.

He was the President-elect in 1960, ushering in the Crucible Sixties as did Abraham Lincoln in 1860, one hundred years before him. Both these men had much in common from a number angle. Honest Abe's cornerstone letter is an A, which vibrates to *1*, while New Frontiers Jack's name starts with J, also a *1* letter. The *1* is symbolical of the emancipator and the innovator. Their Middle Cycle numbers digit to the key-letters of their surnames. The L of Lincoln synchronizes to his birthday *12* (*3*). Mr. Kennedy's key-letter K carries the number *11*. This harmonizes with his day of birth, *29*, reduced to *11*. And there are many more similarities between their scopes, too numerous to take account of here.

NAMES AND NUMBERS

You may hear it said: "I'm a *three*," or "I'm an *eight*." This pertains to the numerical value of the letters in one's name reduced to a single digit. For this number indicates what you really are.

A "ONE" PERSONALITY

The *one* stands for aloneness, for solitude and singleness of purpose. Its influence is extrovert and represents the "I am" consciousness in the Cosmic Rhythm. So naturally the *one* is wholly concerned with self. Pride is a keyword.

If this number rules your personality, you prefer to work alone, in fact, you resent others butting into your schedules, or worse, have a Smart Aleck lord it all over you. You have a single track mind and are endowed with tremendous powers of concentration. As a rule, *one* personalities work rapidly when not interfered with. You detest scattering of your mental forces. Physically you should guard against overdoing things. Remember there are only twenty-four hours in a day. You should also avoid working mentally at night, after the evening meal. Relaxations should be pleasurable, not taxing the brain. Children with this personality number ought not to be allowed to do their school homework at night. Many of this number are poor sleepers, and some may suffer from insomnia.

One personalities are fully conscious of their responsibilities as leaders. This implies initiative, organizing ability, the virtue to make decisions alone and not to be pressured. Your ambition for achievements is boundless. You succeed best when operating from an anchorage. You should be blessed with the courage of a pioneer.

KEYWORDS: Initiative, leadership, originality, creativity,

self-started drive, inspirational, spontaneity, organization and self-sufficiency.

A "TWO" PERSONALITY

One plus *one* equals *two*, which means *one* is no longer alone. This introvert and feminine number works harmoniously and successfully with others. People whose character is ruled by *two* cooperate willingly and complement the rugged individualist in his quest for fame and fortune.

These folk are the balance wheel in the universal rhythm. They avoid going to extremes, preferring to travel the middle lane. As they represent the opposite of *one*, they show opposite traits of character, preferring to remain in the background. If the *two* is your personality number, you do not push yourselves or your interests to the fore, but adapt yourself quickly and without resistance to the forceful egotist. Go-betweens, peacemakers, coordinators and negotiators often boast of a prominent *two* in their number make-ups. Your forte should be tact and diplomacy. You are cautious and can follow a prearranged plan. While you may lack creative ability and original thinking you excel in the "feel" of form and sometimes are remarkable musicians, painters and colorists. The *two* personality succeeds best in partnership with someone else, when functioning as a collaborator or assistant to an inventor or organizer.

KEYWORDS: Tact, diplomacy, coordination, negotiation, collector and appraiser.

A "THREE" PERSONALITY

Was it not Plato, the Greek philosopher, who said of the *three* as the basis for the trine, that it was the most beautiful number symbol, without a flaw? No doubt he was contemplating this number as it follows in the sequence of 1, 2, 3. For the *one* represents the ego, or divine spark of human inspiration. The *two* signifies the soul expression, but the *three* operates on the plane of nature. Therefore this numerical influence has affinity with the moulding into form, such as self-expression, artistic adornment and it strives for perfection. The extension of the personality is always of paramount importance to you, ruled by the *three* vibration.

We mean such trifling things as clothes and fashions, styles in interior decorating or architecture, trivial to many, but all important to you of a *three* consciousness. You feel that the projection of your voice registers high cultural levels, or it should. Even the choice of words counts with you. Hence a literary flair may be your special talent, or a hobby. The rest of the world should go to you *three* personalities and learn from you the art of self-expression. For in these days of commercial externalism, your number vibration has been assigned a more than justified position.

KEYWORDS: Charm, culture, form-perfection, attraction powers, affability, artistic leaning, literary talents.

A "FOUR" PERSONALITY

Why is it that your splendid *four* number is often looked upon askance as "unlucky"—perish the thought—and a humdrum influence? Does it not stand for the Temple Four-Square? Does not your *four* mean partial harvest? It symbolizes the sweat of the brow, to be sure, but do not the laws of the universe emphasize that one never gets something for nothing and that one reaps as one has sown? Your *four* symbol belongs to the earth element, it has affinity with substance and shadow. But why dwell on the shadows alone? You understand that substance is a fascinating thing, and that our planet is composed of matter. Therefore you know how to deal with the simplest, most prosaic, human problems: room and board, health, clock-punching jobs, and most of all, the balancing of the budget. You deserve full credit for not wandering the visionary, unpractical paths of daydreaming, but you usually stick to the factual equation that 2×2 equals your *four*.

In its higher octave your number is related to technical details, to logic and legal facts, to plain and simple methods, to mechanical skill, science and inventions.

KEYWORDS: Facts, logic, practicability, sobriety, partial harvests, perfection of form.

A "FIVE" PERSONALITY

You are the weathercock in the scheme of existence. You can change your direction—mentally and emotionally—with the wind. This versatility could be ingrained in your basic character, as a restless, volatile temperament. But you may be basically a steadfast person, though your character is ruled by the *five*. Then the reason for your changeful destiny pattern could be a buffeting about by the unaccountable vicissitudes of life. Be this as it may, the fact remains that you *five* personalities, men or women, are often denied the pleasures of the fireside, for sudden and unexpected changes could hit you like a bolt from the blue.

The intrinsic quality of your soulhood stands for variety. It could result in swift pivotal turning-points, shift of scene, travel, even globe-trotting—and that mysterious attraction power called "sex appeal."

KEYWORDS: Magnetism, nervous tension, inspirational ideas, restlessness, curiosity, inventiveness, salesmanship.

A "SIX" PERSONALITY

Whether you travel into outer space investigating the "gender" of the heavenly bodies or whether you stick close to earth in quest of sex—you can't escape the *six*. It's identified with the "mating instinct." No matter how celibate you may be by instinct or by philosophy, sometime, somehow, the *six* will hit you with the desire to marry and to enjoy the comforts of a home. For in this mysterious rhythm of life ultimately your number influence will come around propelling you with a desire for adjustment—domestic adjustment, that is. The *six* means love of home and family and friends, sociability, domesticity. Being utterly lacking in the Bohemian touch, you are basically rooted in respectability according to conventional standards. *Six* means 3+3, so logically it combines a desire for self-expression with a reaching for the opportunity for all outlets—the stage, concert platform, the speaker's rostrum. Joy and inspiration permeate your expression, with the result that the world's great entertainers and performers show a prominent *six* in their numberscope. Responsibility for home and family also is symbolized by your *six* consciousness.

KEYWORDS: Association, partnership, domesticity, personal adjustments, marriage and divorce, a permanent home.

A "SEVEN" PERSONALITY

With poetic license, we like to state that the "quality of numbers is not strained," for the *one* and the *seven* suggest solitude and aloneness. But there is a difference. The *one* is masculine, positive and active and prefers individualism when projecting energy. The *seven*, on the other hand, is negative and passive. Therefore you of a *seven* personality may become a channel through which creative energy can flow, for *seven* is receptive and intuitive and completely inductive. This vibration is often likened to the temple atmosphere of worship and there is little affinity with the concepts of reality. Your number *seven* is the ideal vibration for the philosopher, the metaphysician and the priest. Profanely considered, *seven* is represented by the statesmen, for great suavity, diplomacy and nervous poise are virtues of your type.

Furthermore, you can hold information without betraying in the least that you are in possession of important top secrets. So what number would be more appropriate for the detective and the FBI man? You 7 people are by nature secretive about your own personal affairs and keep your thoughts and emotions to yourselves. Being essentially introverted, you do not mingle readily with the gay rabble and the boisterous merrymakers. You prefer to delve into the mysterious wonders of untouched nature rather than waste your time in social frivolities.

KEYWORDS: Receptivity, passiveness, secretiveness, diplomacy, and silence.

AN "EIGHT" PERSONALITY

The origin of the figure 8 can be traced to two squares placed diagonally on top of each other, which resulted ultimately in the two circles composing the present figure 8. The square symbolizes the *4*, hence figuratively considered the *8* is twice *4*. This is a very material vibration. If you will, consider that it tops the concord of *2*, *4* and *8*, all earth element numbers, over which the number *8* rules supreme. You *eight* people never do things in a picayune manner. You conceive financial schemes or commercial projects in a big way. You reach for top positions where responsibility is great and where you will not be restricted by material limitations. It is the perfect number for the banker, the top executive, or president of vast enterprises. Naturally you people with a strong *eight* consciousness can envision large sums of money, can handle million-dollar ventures and conceive of business undertakings on a gigantic scale. This calls for fiscal mastership and those among you who can demonstrate such ability should ultimately reap your just reward: We mean you get rich! An *eight* personality can enjoy life and happiness only after complete economic freedom has been achieved. It has sometimes been stated that *eight* personalities worship God in the bank.

KEYWORDS: Honor, prestige, conservatism, wealth, business acumen, financial genius.

A "NINE" PERSONALITY

This number vibration represents group-consciousness. You *nine* personalities reach for the public and function well before large audiences. You dislike the confines of a narrow circle, the small-town atmosphere and suburban minds which try to hold you down to orthodox attitudes. Sooner or later, the *nine* native will find himself confronting the world at large—universal souls and cosmpolitan settings suit well the fast speed and big orbit in which you function. This number tops the concord of *3, 6, 9,* dealing with human values. But being the culmination of this scale you must remain impersonal in relation to individuals. You may reach out for the many in the written word, through music or in the field of art. Often you have an important message to give by which the multitude are reached and comforted. As this number *9* does not claim affinity with the earth element, your fame means more to you than material reward—and riches are not what you seek. Possessions do not tempt you. But to realize that you have reached the top of the ladder of artistic expression or of some intellectual pinnacle makes life worth living for you *nine* personalities.

KEYWORDS: Universalism, fame, artistic acheivement, idealism, global consciousness.

MASTER NUMBERS "11" AND "22"

The master numbers are double numbers and are reduced to a single digit only in rare instances. The *1+1* remains as *11*, while the twice *2* as a double number stays a *22*. However, we want to stress that the *11* is by no means a higher octave of the *1*, nor is the *22* an intensification by octave of the *2*.

These mysterious master numbers *11* and *22* present a high-frequency in human mental equipment akin to sublime genius. It follows logically that few individuals can harmoniously assimilate these hyper-potential currents. In most cases their vibrations short-circuit and are in the ultimate action destructive. Many crackpots and eccentrics struggle all their lives with the too-challenging *11* vibration, while the alcoholic and dope addict strives for that escape we often associate with a *22* challenge. The *11* is the symbol of the emancipator, the inventor, and the iconoclast, for this number represents the element "air," reflecting abstract mentalism. The *22* is an emotional force, highly intuitive and inspirational. It is represented by the element "water," the symbol of the creative artist. It functions as a channel for the interpretive performer.

Both number types are utterly unorthodox and unconventional and "a law unto themselves." They are imbued with cosmic consciousness—representing divine law—but rebel against the narrow confines of man-made codes of behavior.

AN "ELEVEN" PERSONALITY

The *11* is a number which extends itself beyond the scope of the *1—9* limits and reaches for a global consciousness far ahead of the ordinary type of human mentality. Understandably, *eleven* personalities do not get along well with fellow-beings, because it is difficult for them to telescope their viewpoints to the level of the conventional man or woman. On the other hand, the *eleven* persons are rarely fully appreciated by others. They find few "souls akin" among their associates. But life compensates. The *eleven* native, when evolved and living on the constructive side of his soul, is adept in handling materials. He deals with situations and events and loves to delve into the hidden mysteries of nature. For this reason, *11* is often called the "number of revelation" by numerologists.

Let me cite the fabulous achievements of Benjamin Franklin, Leonardo da Vinci and other titans of the mind whose *eleven* consciousness caused them to delve below the surface of the manifested world of their civilization.

KEYWORDS: Analysis, inspiration, moral courage, discrimination, inventiveness, revelation.

A "TWENTY-TWO" PERSONALITY

Sometimes we feel sorry for those unfortunate ones who are saddled with a *22* in their numberscope, yet are neither able to exploit this master vibration nor able to cope with it.

For the *22* is highly emotional. If people lack talent and willpower and education they will soon become mixed up in the tangle of their own criss-cross desires and passions. Only those who live on the high plane in human evolution can consider the *22* a blessing bestowed upon them by a kindly Fate. Then we meet up with a genius and possibly with one of the immortals.

Let me refer in this instance to the composers Frederic Chopin (February 22nd) and Richard Wagner (May 22nd) both born on the 22nd day of their birth months. They were channels of inspiration endowed with individualistic creativity that defied an established trend. Hence they became forerunners of a new era in music. In the field of commerce and industry the *22* represents enterprises on a gigantic scale (Lucius Boomer, hotelman, August 22nd), coast-to-coast business organizations, chain stores, even undertakings of an international scope (Millikan, physicist, March 22nd). But there again the danger of over-expansion lurks, in extending tentacles of their daring business too far. Confusion, fiscal chaos and ultimate collapse are the consequences, aptly symbolized by the Tower of Babel. Serge Rubenstein and Ivar Kruger are pitiful examples of over-optimistic business expansions, which soon caught them in their own trap and ended in bankruptcy and spectacular economic disaster.

KEYWORDS: Enthusiasm, idealism, creativity, vision, cooperation, faith.

MISSING LETTER NUMBERS

When a letter number is missing in a name it is an indication that the ego must encounter serious handicaps in life. Challenges will have to be met of the nature which this number, though absent, represents. Study your own name and find out what letters you have missing, for this is a guide-post to the lessons you must learn and will have to master sooner or later. It is a danger signal which warns you to watch your step and avoid the pitfalls indicated along your pathway.

As our example we offer the name of a world-famous and extremely successful film actress, Elizabeth Taylor, born February 27, 1932.

$$\underline{\begin{matrix} \text{E L I Z A B E T H} \\ \text{5 3 9 8 1 2 5 2 8} \\ 7 \end{matrix}} \quad \underline{\begin{matrix} \text{T A Y L O R} \\ \text{2 1 7 3 6 9} \\ 1 \end{matrix}} \quad \text{total: } \underline{8}$$

LETTER BREAKDOWN

1) 2	2) 3	3) 2
4) —	5) 2	6) 1
7) 1	8) 2	9) 2

Miss Taylor's name is composed of two *1*'s, three *2*'s, two *3*'s, two *5*'s, one *6*, one *7*, two *8*'s, and *two 9*'s.

The *four* is her missing letter number. This is her challenge.

It would seem that this girl has everything life can bestow

upon a human being. The 2 is in the majority. It is the most feminine of all numbers and explains why she is the essence of feminine pulchritude and glamor. The 2 does not suggest tomboyish or boisterous mannerisms and does not picture a gal in blue-jeans and slouchy, mannish sweat-shirts. Soft fabrics and elegant lines are indicated for her clothes, and a chic silhouette for hair-do. The 8 is a material power indicator. Miss Taylor will never want or have to face the poorhouse; and the 9 suggests globe-trotting and world fame. The 3 and 1 combination bestows a scintillating, magnetic personality and histrionic ability.

But the "missing 4" is a warning that Miss Taylor must take good care of her health. Her physical constitution is pictured as frail.

YOUR MISSING NUMBERS

All missing numbers in any name give a message, a negative one of what the obstacles are that must be overcome and a positive one, for it shows the ways and means of how such challenges can be successfully met, how victory can be achieved.

A Missing "1"

This is a difficult handicap to overcome, for the ego lacks the necessary drive and aggressiveness to meet obstructions to his plans successfully. His aspirations in life will encounter barriers, perhaps parental opposition to a chosen vocation, or to a desired mode of life. Stronger wills are apt to oppress him and control his life, if not his pocket-book. The nature is unstable which may stem from an inferiority complex and a weak desire to please everyone.

If the numberscope is debilitated elsewhere with many vacillating influences the person is over-cautious, even distrustful, lacking in ability to judge character, and is hesitant about making decisions. When he finally embarks on a completely new and untested venture it is frequently too late. Then Failure beckons.

ADVICE: Develop a firm stand after investigating all facts. Strengthen your powers of volition. Do not permit your vacillating or hesitant attitude to turn into unreasonable obstinacy.

A Missing "2"

You should overcome a tendency to be impatient. Do not expect too quick results from your efforts. Obedience to a cause and cooperation with other people will be required of you. Do not rebel. Often such persons overlook small items in financial expenditures or even in psychological situations. You can salvage many problems with tact. Your failure to be punctilious about keeping appointments may be interpreted as arrogance. A "missing 2" personality often finds destiny pushing him or her into touchy situations that call for shrewd sagacity and insight into the motives of people who cause delays. Curb over-sensitiveness. You are not the center of the universe and must learn to forgive and forget thoughtless remarks by others. Another foible is your insistence on consideration for your feelings, yet you yourself can be blatantly brusk and tactless.

ADVICE: Learn to be impersonal. Have a universal outlook on immediate problems. Don't try to keep up with the Joneses and avoid becoming an imitator, or even a plagiarist. Banish fear thoughts. Stop feeling sorry for yourself.

A Missing "3"

The desire for self-expression is often curbed by lack of talent or the opportunity to give vent to such impulses. You must understand that abilities and talents need study and practice. No expert falls from the sky. Develop self-confidence and overcome your aversion for mingling with fellow-beings. Get stimulation in social intercourse and from your contact with friends who have artistic leanings and intellectual interests. Focus on worthwhile aims, for a "missing 3" often becomes a chatterer and a gossip. Cultivate eloquence with words. Develop a hobby—music, literature or art.

ADVICE: Your lack of special talents may drive you to over-emphasize your outer appearance and to lay stress on the trivial things in life. Steer clear of the temptation to become an externalist. Moods and irritability are to be curbed, for they stem from your sense of frustration. Go for the things in life that cause you fun and relaxation: dancing, music, sports or artistic pursuits.

A Missing "4"

Here is an obvious shunning of details when application to a task is demanded of you. Minor issues confuse you and you want to run away from drudgery and unimaginative routine. You look upon strenuous concentration on specific jobs as a hardship. Menial work especially is distasteful to you. You look for a way out of the physical preparations necessary for most any kind of an accomplishment. Filing and classifying chores are taboo, and frequently your affairs get into chaos from which you avoid extricating yourself. Above all, your physical health needs constant attention, and your best way to build up a strong constitution is regularity in your work schedules, relaxation which does not abuse the physical self, and out-door recreation and exercise.

ADVICE: Your challenge will teach you that the "sweat of the brow" is the basis for truly worthwhile accomplishments. Nothing can be achieved the easy way. Don't shirk sacrifices on the way to a laudable goal. Application to detail is essential no matter what your vocational ambition in life may be. Ask yourself the simple questions: Am I lazy and indolent? Do I shirk responsibilities? Then start out doing something the hard way.

A Missing "5"

The 5 is a much-misinterpreted number. Most numerologists associate it merely with sex and the gratification of the senses. This is the case only when many earth numbers turn the mind of the ego toward animalistic pleasures. But when the 5 is coupled with intellectual influences, its nature is imaginative and creative. When this number is missing we meet a personality that shies away from life's experiences. The mind is intolerant toward others who enjoy living life wholeheartedly. A complete lack of imagination causes such egos to fear progress in human unfoldment. Do not avoid running the gamut of human experiences. Seek adventure and learn the facts of life. Sooner or later you will find your destiny to place you in situations when psychological understanding of your fellow-beings will be demanded of you. Do not go through life with your eyes blindfolded. Adjust quickly to changes. Be pliable in mind.

ADVICE: Meet emergencies with cheerful mental resilience.

Try to learn essential traits of humanity from your fellow-men. Do not shrink from situations which seem peculiar to you, or even unworthy of your cultural and social level. Learn from the world in which you live the virtue of compassion.

A Missing "6"

The keyword for a 6 is adjustments. This then will be your challenge in life: to learn to adjust yourself to environmental changes and to adapt your own personality to the difficult, rigid minds with which your destiny is bound to confront you. You may have to live with people whose intrinsic nature is opposed to your ideals and ideas. Domestic responsibilities frequently press upon you, not only on your pocket-book but also on your freedom of motion. Then do not rebel because you are tied down utterly against your likes and desires. Your greatest cross is that "unfinished business" problem. You may never have the time, the inclination nor the ready cash to see your aspirations through to a finish. Do not force your interpretation of problems and opinions on those you contact in your daily life. Do not refuse to shoulder unfair obligations. Stop trying to argue with Fate.

ADVICE: Self-righteousness and over-positivism are your great shortcomings. Your smugness and dictatorial demeanor makes it difficult for others to enjoy living with you. Therefore learn to respect the individual and his or her own standards and attitudes. Don't try to make other people over. You need love in life, get it by adjusting to surroundings and adapting yourself to people.

A Missing "7"

This is the supreme mystic number and when it is absent in your name you are likely to be opposed to the various "ologies" and even to the metaphysical schools of philosophy. On the other hand, you could go off the deep end of psychism and lose your perspective of the realities that these forms of occult learning offer. Strive for a harmonious blending between reality and metaphysical thought.

Psychologically considered, the absence of the 7 indicates that you are apt to repress your emotions. You shrink from demonstrating your affections, stand aloof from human intercourse and seek solace in solitude. Yet, way down deep in your soul you crave love and friendship, for you need the warmth of emotional display. This coldness of heart is frequently the result of foolish pride and a fear of finding your affections repulsed or treated lightly. You take yourself and your feelings altogether too seriously. Thus you build up a barrier between yourself and your fellow beings, suffer from repression complexes and ultimately seek that precarious form of escapism: Demon Rum.

ADVICE: Overcome emotional introversion by expressing your talents and displaying your educational training. Voice your opinions—even those that may clash with accepted concepts. Be lavish with your affections. Display your intuitional foresight to advantage. Engage in some form of occult wisdom. Bring to the fore the hidden beauty and opalescent warmth of your soul.

A Missing "8"

This is a material vibration and if you lack this number in your name you may have a tendency to fear dying in the poorhouse. You overestimate material problems. You may worry where your next meal is coming from and how the rent will be met. But extremes are also in evidence here. You may belong to the group of wastrels whose improvidence in economical matters causes them to be perpetually one foot ahead of the sheriff. The axiom: "Neither a borrower nor a lender be" applies to the "missing 8" personality. It is well for you to stay clear of the extremes in destructive financial attitudes: miserliness and cupidity on one hand and recklessness in expenditures on the other. Your wrong sense of value is bound to make you miserable because of the limitations it introduces into your life.

ADVICE: Do not worship the Golden Calf of material possessions. Let not the mighty dollar influence your decisions and actions. Stop thinking of mere money as the ultimate of happiness. Do not make a secret worship of your pay envelope. Let no one butt into your economic affairs.

A Missing "9"

This is the easiest of all challenges to meet. For the 9 stands for human values and a de-focussing of your own puny and picayune problems. Widen your mental horizon and turn your attention to the world at large and the misery that prevails there. Then compare your own destiny with that of those worse off than yourself. The *9*, being of an emotional quality, demands demonstration of your own sympathies toward others. Hardheartedness presents a challenge for kindness. An unfeeling attitude toward fellowmen is a drawback of your "missing *9*" personality. Learn to show appreciation of the suffering of friends and relatives. Become interested in their activities and problems.

Sometimes you refuse to help others from a fear of becoming involved. You hesitate to assist or do favors for others in order not to be drawn into unpleasant perplexities, if not unfavorable publicity.

ADVICE: Call to the fore your affectionate nature before one disappointment after another drives you to become a cynic and a scoffer. Learn to exercise your emotions. Keep up with current events and develop interest in international affairs. Stop thinking of "What's in it for me" when you do a good deed.

COMPENSATIONS

Speaking of the *9* as a missing number, we admit it is a rare occasion. For when checking up on elements in a name from a number point of view we find that the *9* and the *5* are rarely missing. The challenges of the missing numbers *9* and *5* therefore have not often puzzled humanity. The *3* and the *6*—which belong to the expression concord of *3, 6, 9*—also are usually represented in the letter-number graph of a name.

However, the most serious challenges arise from a missing *7*, and we conclude that the appalling negative thinking which prevails in the world today is due to the challenge of the introverted missing *7*. The *8* also is frequently missing with its overemphasis on economic problems, its tendency toward gross materialism.

"Fair to middling" are the absentees *2* and *4*—practical influences that may be considered a balance wheel to steady the other restless, moveable number vibrations.

But no matter what's missing in your name, console yourself with the fact that these numbers can be compensated by other aspects in your name. Let's say you lack a *3* and find several *5*'s represented in your name. This indicates that originality and inventiveness and creativity along artistic lines could fully make up for the lack of the self-expression number *3*.

If you find, on the other hand, a crowding of numbers 9 or 5 in your name chart, you should search for a 4. This practical, sober and steadfast influence could function as an anchor to hold you down and stabilize that too-much vacillating usually plaguing these over-active personalities.

The 4 is often needed by other numbers in a lopsided name analysis. Like a medical man, it comes to the rescue to help you adjust disturbing conditions in your destiny pattern, which, in turn, manifest themselves as grave problems in your life.

But when all is said and done, there remains this vital fact: Never judge just one number aspect and pluck it out of the entire picture. Always judge any influence, whether predominant or absent, in relation to the other numbers in your name. Numerology is not fatalistic. Your name in correlation to your Path of Destiny is merely an instrument for you to play upon. It is up to you to produce a harmonious melody of your life.

NAME CHANGES

Should you change your name? Why not, if you want to! Think of all the girls who have added their husbands' to their own maiden names for better or worse. Men, too, are known to have attempted to improve their destiny by changing their names for business reasons. A talented young executive was christened Owen. He added a middle initial, a D, and operated in life with the legal signature Owen D. Young. It turned out beneficial for him in money matters as well as increasing his business and political prestige to international proportions.

Sometimes one experiences an uncontrollable aversion toward one's baptismal name. A friend of mine was tagged with the biblical Thaddeus. This name provoked much mirth and a lot of fun-poking on the part of his schoolmates and later of his co-workers. He changed to "Thad," and felt much happier with this abbreviation. Certainly it was quite profitable, for he never wanted or ran into any unpleasant mix-ups but led a fairly comfortable, healthy life.

Nicknames too are very important. Sometimes Dick stems from Richard and Jake from Jacob. These nicknames ought not to be overlooked but should be compared with the baptismal name. It is often found that such abbreviations give power to an original name, and supply certain number aspects the original baptismal name did not emphasize.

Another reason for change is a hard-to-pronounce foreign name. Many refugees have come to our shores with tongue-twisters for names, and a legal Americanizing of their name proved desirable for simplification purposes. Whether this turns out to be an improvement or a detriment in their destiny pattern only their complete original name compared with their birthdates can reveal.

Pen-names have always been in vogue. In the olden days when women had neither suffrage nor the right to earn their living with a career, it seemed imperative to select a man's name for a pen-name. A slip of a French girl (born July 1, 1804) was baptized Aurore Dupin. She had the inner compelling drive to become a writer, but being a woman presented a lot of stumbling blocks to fame. So she changed her name to George Sand and made the ranks of celebrities. Her birthday, July 1, 1804, with a *3* for her Path of Destiny, is indicative of literary talents. George Eliot is another writer who was hiding her maiden name under a masculine pen-name.

Artists, too, especially in journalism, sometimes adjust their baptismal names to something more euphonious and "catchy," which may have caused Leroy Ripley to operate as Robert Ripley. Just look about in show business and you will find many celebrities functioning happily and successful with either nicknames or abbreviated first names. Surnames, too, are frequently changed.

I once engaged a talented, pretty young singer as vocalist with my band. She was born Elizabeth Thornburg, February 26th, 1921. This name was utterly unsuitable for a singer with a band and, as I was already then sold on numerology, I gave her a completely new name:

$$\underset{9}{\underline{B\ E\ T\ T\ Y}} \quad \underset{8}{\underline{H\ U\ T\ T\ O\ N}} \quad \text{Total: } \underline{8}$$

This total *8* of her name synchronized with her middle cycle, the Cycle of Productivity. But the many *2*'s in her name vibrated to her birth month number 2 (February) which represents her first or Formative Cycle. Betty started her brilliant career in show business while still in her teens. But it was not until she had reached her Cycle of Productivity, ruled by the *8* (birthday, 26, total *8*) that she hit the jackpot and big time as a film star and a popular comedienne.

When selecting a name for Betty, I concentrated on increasing the power of her numberscope and bringing out the beneficial aspects of her destiny. As Elizabeth Thornburg she might have been successful in grand opera, had she been endowed with a dramatic voice. But the name I gave her proved popular and suitable for the entertainment world of show business she selected for her very own vehicle.

Vocational suitability was the springboard from which I proceeded when making up her name. The rules of numerology also had to be considered.

This is the rule you should apply when changing your own name: A name "letter total" should correlate to the number vibration of either the Cycle of Productivity, or the number of the Path of Destiny. Betty Hutton has a name total 8, which dovetails with her middle cycle 8. This is a vibration of fame and riches, but it does not necessarily promise personal happiness. Often you see talented young stars flash across the horizon of fame, but their lives are lonely and loveless.

Ask yourself when changing your name: "What is it I want to achieve in my life?" Are you looking for a happy marriage and congenial companionship? Is it economic security you're after? Or do you wish to pursue a career successfully? These aims must be drawn into consideration if you wish to originate a beneficial name for yourself. Better still, we advise, let a competent numerologist do the job for you.

IV

Numbers and Philosophy

SYNTHESIS AND ASSEMBLATIONS

As we stated in the beginning we did not intend this volume to present an exhaustive textbook on the number science, for there is no room here for the various complex ramifications of this technique, such as the Intermediate Period Table, the Ruling Passions, Pinnacles and the profoundly mystical Karmic Lessons. These are topics the ambitious student may take up later, after he has mastered all the rules given here—and they are fundamental.

But even though you may plan to use this information on numerology merely for your own convenience or to help your friends, we feel you should be acquainted with some of the essentials of interpretation required for the analysis of numberscope.

Numerology is divided into two major facets:

a) CHARACTER ANALYSIS. This is based on the full baptismal name.
b) INTEPRETATION OF THE LIFE PATTERN. This is revealed by the birthdate.

Points *a* and *b*, when combined, result in *c*:

c) THE FORECAST. This is based on both combined—the name, letter total and the birthdate numbers.

These are the springboard from which a forecast indication can be made. For the name reveals the equipment of the ego with which to meet the exigencies of life's struggle, and the birthdate is a hint, periodically, from what angle opportunities to exercise this character instrument may be expected.

What good are talents when the opportunities to use them are lacking in one's destiny? Numerology will point out to you at what time major occasions for the application of your aptitudes and abilities may arise. Bear in mind, however, that you should treat a forecast merely as an indication of the nature of the experiences an individual may have to undergo at a certain period in his or her life.

Is this experience that's indicated for a person in the nature of an economic harassment? Are emotional vortexes presaged that could mould the soul in the cauldrons of heartbreaking disappointments? Or is the physical constitution undergoing a stress of depleted vitality? If the latter, remember that you cannot under any circumstances predict forms of illnesses, for this is apt to get yourself and numerology into a hassle with the American Medical Association.

CHARACTER ANALYSIS

The beginner is often inclined to negativize number interpretations when stumbling over a conglomeration of letter-numbers of the same kind in a numberscope.

Take the much-maligned 4 as an example. The tyro is apt to hurl dire judgment at the 4-afflicted person by proclaiming want, failure, death in a poorhouse or a sanitarium for him. This is a grave error. Never just pluck out one number aspect of an analysis and judge from this alone. All numbers must be adjuged in relation to their complete number association and not themselves.

You will have learned by now that the pleasure-loving 3 and the ever-restless 5 are inclined to scatter even the most precious talents or vocational aptitudes a person may be endowed with. Then woe unto him or her if the 4 is lacking! For in such a number-total the cornerstone 4 acts like a cubic block upon the scattery 3 and 5 may be grounded. The 4, by the same token, is practically indispensable to the inspirational 11. Those who have knowingly changed their names by adding 3 to their 11 were wise in their endeavor to exploit superior occupational endowments.

The great French actress Sarah Bernhardt changed her "key" from Rosina (4) to Sarah (11) and was smart to hold on to the original 1's in her name to supply the drive and the inexhaustible ambition which marked her career. Still the 4 operated in the background as a perfectionist influence, for this famous woman was indefatigable in her research of the Gallic beauty in the French language through constant practice. To hear her speak was pleasurable to the ears even of those who did not know one word from another of the French language. Do not indulge in the fallacious optimism that master-numbers—*11* or *22*—promise top channels of fame and fortune. They couldn't, without the *4* to cement their efforts through hard work and persistent application with one specific objective in view. This is synthesis, plain and simple. The dictionary states: "Synthesis is the combination of separate elements into a complete whole."

Numbers complement each other. There are missing links in any number pattern, as a rule. You must learn therefore that missing numbers, either in a name or a birth date, can be supplemented by other strongly-posited numbers.

Again take the *3* as a missing number in this case. The *3* supplies the "gift of gab." But suppose a journailst, or someone who wishes to become a writer, finds the *3* missing in his or her numberscope. Should that be cause for worry? Certainly not! Many *5*'s and some *9*'s in the pattern will fully complement this void, and as you have previously read, *5*'s and *9*'s are rarely wanting in a scope. The talent for flowery language may be missing, we admit, but the gifted journalist may have tremendous original ideas or a manner of presentation that smacks the reader between the eyes. These various aptitudes may fully compensate for the missing *3*, indicative of the avalanche of words.

Again when you find a lot of numbers of one kind and none of another the native may be a lopsided person. With many *5*'s he could function excellently in the outer office or as a high-pressure salesman. But someone else will have to supply the necessary number influences to function as the ideal desk executive. Here the Law of Opposites operates in that a suitable partner should be found to round out a set-up for success in a given business organization.

This is a study by itself, called Number Affinities.

ASSEMBLATIONS

The word assemblation is derived from the verb "to assemble" and that is exactly what it signifies—to assemble three or more number values of different element or influence in one given numberscope, which could be for better or worse as regards the person in whose pattern this assemblation is found.

Take the *3—5—8* as an example. This is a very advantageous combine from a material point of view. Suppose the native with such an assemblation meets with catastrophic reversals and is completely wiped out financially. Here is what might happen according to this combination of numbers.

The 5 would hurl this individual into despair, for the 5 is pivotal and moodish, and often functions at the emotional extremes. Therefore, the 5 consciousness would be apt to chase him through the Slough of Despond. But only for a short while. Then the 3 will raise its head with its incorrigible optimism and will come to the rescue with original ideas, a happy way out of troubles. A fresh look at the wrecked conditions of a previous economic situation may result. Hope and new courage will soon swell the brest of the misfortune-smitten individual.

Last, but not least, beckons the 8, "of the earth, earthy," belonging to the most staid of all elements. Remember then, that the 8 is twice 4, and that the hidden number in this assemblation is 4—the willingness to apply one's self anew to some different arduous tasks. The 8 also bestows a subconscious sense of value—of where the round and rolling dollars may be caught, and quickly! Soon enough this 3—5—8 personality may find himself in quest of another fortune, grasping at the first opportunity his destiny pattern presents and quickly forgetting his past losses.

Another advantageous assemblation is the 3—6—9 combine, which operates on the plane of talents and artistic gifts, or techniques in the field of crafts and skills. Here again the 3 would function as the element of creativity, when a phase of a career is shattered. Some inspirational thought may suddenly flash through the mind of this individual. But now the Paths of Destiny differ. Instead of a 5 we find the 6: cooperation, adjustment and collaboration. A friend or patron may suddenly present himself and come to the rescue of this skilled craftsman or artist. Then there beckons the 9, for he had already established a reputation for his ability, even if only to a limited circle of those in the know of his particular craft. A new life opens itself up to this person, a new career avenue looms before him, and life goes on in rose-colored visions.

These are the Soldiers of Fortune who can take the count of 9—and get up when the 10 is heard. That is why you find people—and you will have met some of them, no doubt—who have bravely weathered the vicissitudes of life, who have taken it on the chin, got up and started anew from scratch for a bigger success than ever before. They charged their previous misfortunes to experience and came out better men or women.

The 3 is responsible for optimism and that get-up spirit, for it is an emotional, though cheerful, number. The 5 in our first example pertains to opportunities and the 6 in our second example indicates patronage, or a friend or another fellow-being to come to the rescue. The *8* is a financial life-buoy, whereas the *9* indicates public acclaim, or a favorable reputation.

But not all assemblations are helpful and encouraging. Some present themselves as serious stumbling blocks along the Path of Destiny.

Take the *2–4–7* combination. When a person with such a number-conglomerant is floored by the hand of fate, he will find it difficult to extricate himself from his reversals. There is a deeply-hidden psychological reason for this downcast persistency. The *2*, as you have learned, is already submissive to no matter what Life may have to offer. Therefore these people should constantly strive to muster sufficient morale to fight back and overcome opposition, according to the adage: "If you don't lick life, life will lick you."

Certainly the *4* and the *7* are no assets if you wish to become a "Get-Rich-Quick Wallingford." But they are splendid stimulation for anyone who is after the Nobel Prize for scientific discoveries or who wants to write the Great American Novel or concentrate on a musical composition. Any task which requires inviolate and absolute seclusion, such as a laboratory or an artist's studio, is favored by this assemblation: *2, 4* and *7*.

For *7* personalities are endowed with mental concentration, the *4* lends a sense for minute detail essential in scientific research, while the *2* has the patience of Job to try again when initial attempts have failed.

May we remind you here of Madame Marie Curie, born November (*11-2*) 7th. All numbers have a constructive aspect; some may encourage going after that grand kill on the Stock Market, others again beckon with recognition along lines of mental or artistic pursuits.

Assemblations are welcome boosts in the baffling vicissitudes of Life, and they can prove hurdles in the race with Destiny too high for some people to negotiate.

In concluding I would like to draw your attention to the positional value of certain letter numbers. These are:

The Cornerstone
The Key
The Key Letter

All of them pertain to the original baptismal name of a person.

THE CORNERSTONE: This is the first letter of the first baptismal name. Let's take for our example the name of Mary Margaret McBride. The M of Mary would be her cornerstone. This letter vibrates to 4—as do all the other first letters of her three names, of course. Here again you find the *4* no hindrance on the road to prominence in a chosen field of endeavor, for Mary Margaret reached the top with her radio broadcasts.

THE KEY: This is formed by the sum-total of all the letters of her first baptismal name—namely MARY: M (*4*); A (*1*); R (*9*); Y (*7*). Total: *4-1-9-7* equals *21*, or *3*. This is the number of self-expression through words. And it is Mary Margaret McBride's key to her destiny, especially her occupational avenue.

It is very desirable that you should locate your cornerstone number and your key vibration and interpret them both in the light of your destiny pattern.

THE KEY LETTER is a term frequently bestowed upon the first letter of a surname, like K in Kennedy, or M in McBride, or S in Smith. And it is of highest importance in the struggle with the changes the years present in one's destiny pattern.

Now, let's say you have changed your original baptismal name for some reason or other. How will the new name affect you? The original Cornerstone and Key cannot be completely obliterated. But after a pen-name or professional name has been used for some time, at least through the span of a cycle, the individual will find life to coincide somewhat with this new name vibration. Therefore, we emphasize that a name-change is vital, it could be helpful and has proved itself to be so. But to change a name merely to "have better luck," as it is commonly called, and to think of adding an *8* to one's new name for more money is a grave error. The new name *must* somehow conform to the indications of one's Pattern of Destiny. It cannot supply wealth or advantages of a nature not indicated in the original Life Path.

That is why the change of a name calls for a profound knowledge of the Science of Numbers. It cannot be done in a slipshod manner by a tyro in a wild desire to bring forth golden harvests that just aren't indicated.

But there is nothing wrong with changing a name. It's been demonstrated in the Old Testament, for did not God change the name of Sara to Sarah, of Abram to Abraham? In the New Testament we find Saul returning from the Road to Damascus to change his baptismal name to Paul. Today anyone who joins a Holy Order of the Roman Catholic faith will have to change her or his first name to one given to them when entering a convent or a monastery. Name changes are sometimes obligatory. But the alteration should be scientifically correct in order to be of advantage to the native.

For here again a great truth comes into play: That the rose by any other name remains a rose, and, conversely, the leopard cannot change his spots.

THE ORIGIN OF NUMBERS

Numbers are truly awe-inspiring. There is something sublime about their sequence as it continues on and on into Infinity. Suddenly, when you study them arduously, there is revealed to your mortal mind the humming rhythm of the galaxies, the ebb and flow of Time, and the Law of Periodicity which operates throughout the Universe. John Kepler fittingly called it the "Music of the Spheres."

On our own puny planet, numbers are essential in human existence. They are our tools in daily life we couldn't do without. The inch of the hemline in a seamstress's gown is as vital to her as her needle; the carpenter needs his rule when he wants to cut a plank to size. And what would the delicatessen man do when weighing out foodstuffs on his scales if they did not register accurately the numbers of ounces and pounds. The days of our years and the hours of our days all carry their specific numbers.

We wonder at this tremendous perception of law and order that prevails everywhere in the created world; but even more do we marvel at Man's ingenuity to become aware of this universal system. At what period in evolution did he become number conscious? When did Man learn to count?

Probably during the dawn of civilization, when the human race was in its infancy, Man beheld his image in a silent forest pool. He then may have noted that there were two eyes and two ears in his face, only one mouth to eat with. By the same token, he must have observed the four fingers and one thumb on each hand, and we presume that he started to count on his fingers in child-like fashion.

Historians tell us that Man first used sticks to express a certain amount and that later he used pebbles when sums grew larger. This was particularly true when the "counting table" was invented, which ultimately led the Arabs to establish the decimal system.

We must remember that numbers—either single-digit or several digit ones—have two aspects: the number as such and its glyph. An 8 represents a certain amount of something as a number, but it has also a symbol to represent this amount. Number glyphs were used in all countries of antiquity: Egypt, China, ancient Rome, and Greece, which produced history's greatest mathematician, Pythagoras. He did more than any other philosopher to develop a system of numbers, and he also originated the musical scale.

But it was a stick as a figure that supplied the first number symbol of the scale, namely the *1*. Vertical strokes indicate certain sums of a limited amount. The number *1* as a vertical stroke is found in all languages around the globe.

This symbol of the number *1*, a vertical stroke, represents the divine spark of creation. It is masculine, positive and solitary. We still find this symbol in both the Roman number script as well as in our modern Arabic decimal system.

The 2 definitely originated with the Sumerians, an ancient Mesopotamian race. They used sticks too, but laid them horizontally one over the other, as illustrated in our example. These two sticks were united with a curved line.

The *2* is feminine, the opposite pole of the *1*. It is cooperative, negative, and does not function well solitary.

Our modern *3* also is said to have been invented during the horizontal stick system of the old Sumerians. Again three sticks were united with curved lines.

The *3* is an extension of the *1* and the *2* consciousness of Man, and signifies group awareness. That is why a *3* is vital in someone's numberscope, for it indicates a person's ability to get along with other members of the human society.

The *4* is a material vibration; it represents the grim struggle for existence, the humdrum, unimaginative battle of life. Man soon realized that he had to face climatical rigors and dangers in order to "bring home the grub" for his wife (*2*) and child (*3*). The symbol of the *4*, therefore, is understandably either a cross or a square. Symbolically it means that the soul of Man is crucified on the cross of matter.

But again the ancient Arabs came to the assistance of numerology. As the great mathematicians of their day, they knew well their calculus of the heavens, abstractly so, but also in relation to the earth. They were reputedly most competent astrologers and we cannot blame them for borrowing from planetary symbology for their number glyphs.

They represented the *4* as a cross surmounted by the crescent, which is exactly the symbol of the Great Preserver, the planet Jupiter. This planet signifies material supply.

During the Middle Ages many Hermetic Societies identified the vibrations of the 4 with the Jupiter ray. In fact, they assigned to the Great Jupiter the number 4.

The origin of the figure 5 is a mystery. No one actually knows how or where it came into being. It certainly has a similarity to the symbol of the planet Saturn, always associated with reversals, and as the vibration of the number 5 has a definite pivotal quality, the ancient Arabs are said to have lifted this glyph from the Saturn symbol. However, this theory is a matter of conjecture.

This is equally true of the number 6 as a symbol. Strangely it has been discovered in inscriptions of Indian caves that are as old as three centuries before Christ and still the 6 resembles our present cipher. How it came about is problematic. Perhaps a zero, indicating a bag, with a crescent curving upward from it symbolizes this number of domestic responsibilities, of adjustments and benevolence.

Much more information could be garnered for the origin of the 7, which can be traced to the ancient Chaldeans. They are credited with having been the earliest astrologers, and they were familiar with the circle of the Zodiac. These ancient nature students divided a great circle of the sky not only into constellations but also into 'decans.''

The Chaldeans lived in the plains of Mesopotamia which accorded them an unobstructed view of the sky. The planetary movements and the influences of the planets on their flocks and on human life was their particular study. They could sight the planets with the naked eye, including Saturn, the seventh planet, then the outer planet of our solar system.

The 7 was recognized by these star-gazers of antiquity as a mystic, sacred number. This gave birth to the various sayings pertaining to the number 7, such as the *seven* angels before the throne, the *seven* candlesticks and so on.

Then, too, the Chaldeans were familiar with the shape of the horizon as a complete circle, and the Ecliptic or Zodiac —also as a circle, with its eastern point as its beginning, where all the planets, including the Sun and Moon, rise daily. They counted seven decanates from the rising degree in the east, and drew a line through the seventh decan, as shown in our illustration. This, then, is the rather complex manner in which the 7 came about.

Again we have a parallel between astrological findings and the planetary symbols and numerology. In fact, many of the astronomers—they were originally astrologers—were also numerologists.

There is little argument that the 8 as a cipher is the result of the twice-four, symbolized by two squares superimposed. There is another version which claims that the 8 grew out of curved lines, resembling our modern figure 8. But we do not go along with that for numerological reasons, for the 8 is a mighty material number, suggesting power through money or possessions and advocating the wise handling of the earth's goods. It is therefore an extended *4*, an approach to matter on a broader scale than the consciousness of the plain *4*, with its sense of detail and dogmatic application to work.

9 9 9

The *9* belongs to the concord of the *3—6—9;* and from an angle of interpretation blends well with the *6*, inasmuch as it is a reversed *6*. The crescent again was added to the "bag" of plenty, indicating that the *9* like the *6* represents obligations to others: the *6* to the family and inner circle of one's existence, the *9* to the world and its noble causes.

In its symbol pattern, therefore, the *9* follows the method of the *8*, representing a widening of influence, the *8* from a *4* and the *9* from a *6*.

Numzer glyphs originated independently of each other, and probably simultaneously in some instances, in various parts of the globe. This may account for the numerous conflicting reports of their origin and the multiple different ways these ciphers were written. We've tried to summarize what impressed us as the most likely authentic accounts.

The following illustration shows early European numbers.

I Z Z Y Y L 7 8 9

These are the oldest European number glyphs known, appearing in a manuscript written in Spain in 976. They picture the numbers from *1* to *9*, five of them identical with our modern way of writing numbers: the *1, 6, 7, 8,* and *9*.

Note that the *2* seems upside-down, the *3, 4,* and *5* are unrecognizable. The zero is entirely missing.

Which brings us to the most curious of all numbers: the zero.

The zero has a history all its own. It was unknown to the traders of antiquity, who dealt with the "haves" and not with "have-nots." Even the Great Pythagoras was either ignorant of its existence or else did not feel the need to bother with a zero.

But today it is different, for this number is a vital factor in our fiscal techniques. It is indispensable as a positional factor in our decimal system and in our modern system of banking it is the starting point beyond the *1* and a dividing line between the "black" and the "red" of the ledger. If you overdraw your bank account you will know soon that you have gone below the zero point, where there is nothing left to draw against.

The zero first appeared as a circle representing an empty bag, which indicated nothingness.

The zero is the ground floor of our mathematical system from which we start to climb—upward into the "plus" side or downward into the "minus" side of the ledger, first through the single digit numbers from *1* to *9*. Later we reach the higher octaves of numbers, indicated by adding the zero, such as the *10*, the *20*, the *30* and so on.

This fabulous number of nothingness has its great value as a place indicator in numbers of many digits. It enables mathematicians to deal with enormous figures, into the billions and trillions. This was not necessary during the days when early merchants exchanged goods in their barter system, and they played around with pebbles on their counting tables to figure out small sums.

The zero cannot be overlooked in numerology, for it is indispensable when interpreting the "hidden" number of ciphers of several digits. There are hidden steps to analyze each number, just as there are inner qualities in a human character which do not appear on the surface. Yet in the synthesis of numerology these hidden numbers are important. Take the figure *203*. Its hidden number is *5*, derived from three digit value. In the science of numbers as in anything else you have to penetrate below the surface if you wish to dig deep into the inner meaning of Truth and Spirit Essence.

PLANETS AND NUMBERS

(Astro-Numerology)

No longer do we wonder over the blatant discrepancies that are constantly cropping up in astro-numerology when assigning number influences to planetary rays and vice-versa. Disconcerting contradictions appear in textbooks which necessarily lead the sincere student along the path of confusion.

For instance, two numbers are allotted to the moon, the 2 and the 9. Which one applies? The planet Jupiter is alternately given the value of 3, 7, and 8. Is the ascetic 7 really of the nature of the expansive, optimistic Jupiter?

No, this is all wrong.

However, we have come to realize that these errors are understandable and to a certain extent excusable. For our fine numerology experts know their numbers but are either completely ignorant of astrological fundamentals or know little about them. At the same time, the competent astro-scientist often ignores numbers, except for the planetary periodicities and they do not correlate to numerological values. The springboard from which to operate is the intrinsic vibratory rate of planet and number. They must absolutely dovetail.

Then, too, numbers have many meanings. Take their symbolical interpretation when evaluating human character and human destiny. This differs from their religious significance or their ritualistic one as in the light of cabalistic teachings and the hermetic schools of transcendental magic. One cannot expect these versions to agree with the numerical influences as expounded in this volume.

Yet, since numerology and astrology are both philosophical expressions of cosmology they must of necessity have parallels in vibratory status. The numbers from 1 to 9 can be correlated to basic planetary rays, while the super-planets Uranus and Neptune vibrate to the master-numbers 11 and 22, respectively.

In order to bring system into this confused state of learning, we have exchanged our findings with top professional astrologers, and have succeeded in coming up with a theory we feel is both logical and practical.

The luminaries that dominate the sky are the sun and the moon. They can justly claim the numbers *1* and *2*, as fittingly representing their true planetary nature. All the other planets of our solar system have been examined with equal scrutiny as to "what they stand for," and the corresponding numbers have been assigned to them.

Two numbers cannot properly symbolize one planet, nor can two planets sit pat on one number. It is utterly unscientific.

SUN

Our sun is the center of the solar system around which all the other planets revolve. It is a solar orb radiant with self-effulgence, a mighty fireball that soars through space with dazzling velocity. Typifying Divine energy and the spark of creation, it is the vital principle without which there could be no life.

The masculine gender is represented by Sol, the positive pole and diurnal light. It stands for individuality, rulership and organizing ability. Self-assertion, dignity of bearing and generosity are outstanding traits of the solar character.

SYMBOL: The circle of Eternal life composes the solar symbol. The dot in the middle signifies the incarnated ego.

ONE: All the attributes given to the solar type of humanity also apply to a *one* personality: leadership, aggressiveness, initiative, an egocentric consciousness.

Endocrinolgists have discovered that tribes who are sunworshippers are gonadal types. Their love nature is ardent and their sex-appeal potent. The same is true for *one* persons; there is nothing "wishy-washy" about their affections and friendships.

SUMMATION

Sun: Active, electric, amative, frank, proud, sociable.
One: Creative, original, dominating, loyal, impatient of detail.

MOON

)2

The moon is a satellite of the earth. It shines with reflected glory, for it radiates the reflection of sun's rays. It is cold and dead and without sparkle. Silently it glides through the nocturnal sky, constant in inconstancy—now round and full like a luminous disk, then a tiny sickle and again it disappears completely, as during the nights of the New Moon.

From these attributes you may well gather that the moon is passive and negative, receptive, representing the feminine gender in the universe. Lunar types are impressionable, sensitive and moodish. The moon symbolizes the personality.

SYMBOL: The moon's symbol is the crescent. When the tips of it are directed toward the zenith it is referred to as the Bowl of Heaven. The ancient Persians called Luna the Horn of Plenty.

TWO: Nearly all occult scholars and astro-numerologists agree: The 2 is a perfect number influence to represent the moon. *Two* personalities are gentle and tactful, receptive and cooperative, considerate of fellow-beings. They are not boisterous as the solar (*one*) type, but withdraw into themselves when hurt. Their sulkiness and vacillation are negative traits.

While Sol signifies the spark of creation, the spermatozoon, Luna's line is the curve, the ovum, mystically referred to as the Sacred Chalice of the formative principle.

SUMMATION

Moon: Passive, magnetic, phlegmatic, mediumistic, sensitive.

Two: Adaptable, serving, shy, diplomatic, self-effacing.

MERCURY

☿3

Mercury is a messenger of the mind and must be considered an instrument of expression. However, there is a curious angle to this planet gender-wise: it is neutral. Therefore its gender is determined by the mind that plays upon this instrument. If in close aspect with a masculine orb, such as Sol, or Mars, or Jupiter, Mercury becomes masculine and its expression is mental, Martian or military. But when conjoining a feminine planet, like Venus, its gender becomes feminine also, and the expression verges toward the arts and literature. The famous composers, Tchaikowsky and Chopin had Mercury closely conjunct with Venus—music was the answer! But in the case of Napoleon, born in the fire-sign Leo, we find Mercury also in Leo, a masculine sign, and in an aspect to Jupiter. This accounts for his military genius.

SYMBOL: Fittingly, all *three* basic figures that compose the planetary symbols—the circle, the crescent and the cross—combine to fashion the glyph of Mercury: The circle over the cross, superimposed with the crescent.

THREE: Mercurial types are genuine *three* personalities. They are blessed with the "gift of gab," are witty and intellectual, enjoy popularity and try to spread joy and cheer wherever they go. They are artistic and talented, and take life as it comes.

SUMMATION

Mercury: Inquisitive, volatile, adaptable, active, nervous, mental.

Three: Energetic, cheerful, stimulating, enthusiastic, intellectual.

EARTH

We say "of the earth, earthy" significantly, for of the four elements, fire, water, air and earth, our planet is classified as belonging to the last. Its inhabitants—we mere mortals—are incarnate in matter and our most crucial problems are material ones. For how can the soul rejoice on an empty stomach? We must needs acquit ourselves of our obligations toward ourselves and others no matter how grim the struggle.

It's a case of the "nose to the grindstone" when we grapple with life for the daily bread.

People who live close to Mother Earth, such as farmers, lumbermen, miners or common day laborers experience the rigors of a harsh existence shorn of comfort and beauty; and the clock-punching office workers and shopkeepers know that life on earth is no bed of roses.

SYMBOL: It shows the cross of matter encircled by a ring suggesting the soul's crucifixion in materiality. The earth is the Dark Planet; its gender is feminine.

FOUR: It symbolizes all of these things—menial labor, drudgery and office routine, detail work and mechanical humdrum chores. To slave without joyous inspiration and to groan under the burden of budgeting and skimping and straining to make ends meet are the essence of a *four* destiny pattern.

SUMMATION

Earth: Laboriousness, service, self-denial, discipline, work.
Four: Austerity, obedience, punctuality, meticulousness, method.

MARS

Has it occurred to you that so far in all these pages the term "phallic symbol" has not been mentioned? Well, now it is, in connection with the planet Mars, for the firebrand has affinity with the desire nature, and that includes animal desires. Therefore, fittingly, the 5—which usually stands for "sex" or the "psyche erotica"—is the only number that suggests the intrinsic radiation of Mars. In the chemical make-up of man, Mars rules "pugnacious potassium," which in turn is the direct result of the mechanism of the adrenal gland—the "gland of Mars." Its gender is masculine.

Mars-ruled types are courageous, fiery, impulsive, hot-tempered. But give justice where it is due: they are square-shooters, idealistic, and the Galahads among the planetary types: they show true devotion for a chosen queen of their hearts.

SYMBOL: It's a dart, suggestive of the phallic symbol, superimposed over the circle of divinity. Mars is generally considered a malefic orb, that is when badly afflicted.

FIVE: These personalities are really Martian in nature, loving change, adventure and life experiences. They demand freedom for themselves, are fond of excitement and danger. On the negative side they are like all Mars folk: irresponsible and self-indulgent.

SUMMATION

Mars: Ambitious, explosive, electric, combative, energetic.
Five: Versatile, progressive, spontaneous, daring, clever.

VENUS

True to the nature of Venus, which brings harmony into discord, there has never been any argument about the 6 being its perfect number expression. This is the planet of affability and charm, frequently of physical beauty, but certainly of a prepossessing personality. The social attributes are considerable. Venus-born of either sex are sought after at parties, and often display talent as drawing-room entertainers. For stage, screen and concert platform the zodiac has no equal and their virtues as homemakers and hostesses are exemplary.

SYMBOL: Venus is considered a benefic planet and this is indicated in its symbol by the fact that the circle of divinity is superimposed over the cross of matter.

Six personalities have all of the laudable traits we find in Venusian types: sympathy and understanding, artistic talents, balance and idealism, and the ability to adjust with grace and dignity to no matter what problems arise. Their enthusiasm for domesticity, especially interior decorating, and their knack for flavorsome cooking also are assets that sell these loveable people to the opposite sex. Yes, they *do* like the companionship of friends, including that intimacy in their lives.

SUMMATION

Venus: Affectionate, sociable, magnetic, affable, artistic, loving.

Six: Adjusting, poised, cooperative, talented, conscientious, friendly.

SATURN

♄ 7

In the old magical books Saturn is extolled as a miniature sun, the aristocrat among planets, the magus and philosopher. And, indeed, Saturn-ruled people shun the rabble; they do not care to play the role of glad-hand artist. Work is their vocation, and generally they enjoy their sequestered existence. What causes Saturn to be labelled a malefic planet is the fact that those under its rule are unable to demonstrate affection, yet way down deep they crave love and appreciation. They often go through life unable to attract the thing they want most: true love.

SYMBOL: The cross over the crescent, ruling the personality symbolizes correctly the cross of loneliness these fine people often have to bear. Saturn is a masculine planet.

SEVEN: This personality typifies the Saturn character, being of an ascetic nature, introverted, serious and taciturn. *Seven* as well as Saturn types steer for deep waters only, for the ephemeral does not appeal to them. Wisdom, patience and profundity are their splendid virtues. But they must curb their negative, critical natures.

Financially considered, these people function behind the scenes, and do well as brokers, investment counsellors and bankers. They make conscientious custodians.

SUMMATION

Saturn: Economical, profound, hard-working, solitary, loyal.

Seven: Analytical, conservative, cautious, ascetic, lonely.

JUPITER

♃ 8

Jupiter is the largest planet in our solar system and is called the "Great Fortune."

Jupiter men or women are considered fortunate people and indeed they are, for they are usually endowed with a warmhearted friendliness. They show interest in fellow-beings, including youngsters, and are always ready to lend a helping hand. They are big-minded in business and financial affairs. But it is their optimistic outlook on humans and situations that calls for a response. They believe that ultimate good must result from being a square-shooter.

Yet there is something mysterious about their lives. No matter how tight the pinch in harassing situations, a rescuing angel always seems to turn up at the eleventh hour. Being fond of human nature causes them to have many friends—helpful, influential friends.

SYMBOL: The crescent over the cross signifies that the personality triumphs over adversities. Gender-wise, Jupiter is masculine.

EIGHT: It is their vocational equipment which reflects the *eight* personality in these fine Jupiter types. For they strive for conquest over material problems, try to reach the top in a commercial or financial field, and love to handle big money. *Eight* personalities like the Jupiter folk are splendid organizers and executives, legal aces, and because their religiosity runs along dogmatic lines, they excel in the clergy.

SUMMATION

Jupiter: Noble, just, helpful, generous, discriminating, devout.

Eight: Dependable, enthusiastic, fond of money, efficient, pious.

VULCAN

The French astronomer Leverrier discovered the existence of Vulcan by the perturbations in the orbital movements of Mercury. And according to the Theory of Collision as set forth by Zehnden (physicist, Munich University) it will be the first planet to be drawn into, and absorbed by, the sun.

That means millions of years hence, in terms of cosmic timing.

Vulcan is gaseous and volatile, it is invisible even through a telescope, even when it passes over the disk of the sun. But humans can nevertheless feel its influence, for it races around the sun in about six weeks. Therefore if you feel out of sorts one Blue Monday, and you don't know what accounts for it, blame it all on Vulcan.

SYMBOL: Is in the shape of a V. It stands for unaccountable emotions, vague obsessions of the mind, and utter impersonality. However, deductions as to the true interpretation of this planet's rays on the human soul mechanism are of necessity speculative.

NINE: The *nine* is frequently considered difficult to assimilate by numerologists, because it is not easy for most humans to be impersonal and maintain a global outlook. It is an inspirational force, strives for power on an intellectual plane, and is able to direct operations of groups.

SUMMATION

Vulcan: Exhaustive of self, imaginative, emotionally fluctuating.

Nine: Impersonal, universal, constructive, poised, superior.

URANUS

As may be expected from this explosive orb, its interpretation is constantly subject to heated arguments. Uranus is an electromagnetic dynamo with an alternating current, and gender-wise it is bisexed, both masculine and feminine. It plays a prominent part in the horoscopes of sex deviates and therefore has *erroneously* been labelled the higher octave of Venus, the love planet.

This is incorrect. Uranus is a mental force, the octave of Mercury, the planet of the mind, and its corresponding number is *11*.

SYMBOL: This is composed of two crescents placed back to back, signifying the super-personality of Uranian types. These moons are connected with the cross of matter, over a tiny circle, indicating that the human soul by far dominates the in-carnated ego.

ELEVEN: This is a master-number, just as Uranus is considered a super-planet. It is the ray of the genius, the inventor and the emancipator. If living on a high plane in evolution, these Uranus-*eleven* folk are deeply spiritual, humanitarian, working only for the glory of worthwhile achievements and not for mercenary ends.

SUMMATION

Uranus: Mental, nervous, scientific, inventive, occult.
Eleven: Dynamic, positive, creative, mechanic, mystic.

NEPTUNE

 22

Neptune is the higher octave of Venus, the love planet, and is often called the "Christ-planet" because love here is expanded into a universal scope of love for mankind. These fine Neptune-ruled men or women are channels for superb artistic expressions, music and the dance, and are mediumistic along artistic lines, for they produce beauty inspirationally. But there is another practical side to this planet: it represents plutocratic systems in finance, chain stores, international fiscal ventures, all commercial enterprises on a gigantic scale. Therefore it has a dual quality: baffling artistic and mental productivity and big schemes in the field of industry and commerce.

SYMBOL: Again it is a crescent—the soul symbol—that dominates the glyph, with the cross underneath and a tiny circle. It resembles the trident of Neptune, the God of the Sea, and indeed, Neptune is a "water" element planet. Its gender is feminine.

TWENTY-TWO: These personalities and Neptune's children have much in common. They are visionary and dreamers and think up *big* deeds, and *big* deals. They must learn to keep the balance between inspiration and reality, between pipe-dreaming and practical activities.

SUMMATION

Neptune: Impressionable, inflationary, imaginary, artistic.
Twenty-two: Universal, humanitarian, pious, idealistic.

PLUTO

P 13

The popular comedian Danny Thomas made a very interesting and unconsciously astrologic remark when he stated: "It took me thirteen years to make an overnight success!" For somewhere in his horoscope the planet Pluto must have set off a fuse of fame.

This mysterious planet brings to light the hidden, whatever that "hidden" is, and if you have slaved in the shadows for years, and Pluto comes around, be not surprised if you are elevated into the limelight of recognition.

By the same token, the influence of Pluto could drag a skeleton from the closet and expose it to the glare of a public scandal. For this planet operates at the extremes: wonderful achievement of the human mind on one hand and on the other subversive activities, petty pilfering in the way of brain-picking and plagiarism and gangsterism.

SYMBOL: Like Vulcan, it is the letter P, as so often in astronomy when stellar orbs are designated by a letter.

THIRTEEN: This number is much misunderstood and considered malefic. Indeed it is alien to our terrestrial vibrations, which are mainly signified by the *12*. For the *13* is one of the proportional numbers upon which was constructed the Great Pyramid of Gizeh, which is an astronomical edifice, not a sepulchral monument. Therefore, in its higher octave the *13* becomes the number of the "Anointed"—the *one* set above the dozen.

SUMMATION

Pluto: Subversive, tricky, sinister, inspirational, saintly.
Thirteen: Unaccountable, under-cover, misleading, spiritual.

THE ZODIAC

There are twelve signs in the Zodiac and although they are numbered with Aries, the Ram, the first one, they do not numerically correspond to the months. For instance, January is the first calendar month of the year; it has Capricorn, the Goat, for its zodiacal influence, but only until the 19th day, when the sign changes to Aquarius, the Water-Bearer. Capricorn is the tenth sign of the Zodiac.

The No. 1 sign along the ecliptic, Aries is in force during the fourth month of the year, April, until the 21st. That means a *1*-ruled sign, Aries, falls into the *4*-ruled month, April.

The basic system of numerology according to Pythagoras, as we have explained in this book, takes into account only the calendar month, the day and the year, and the numbers they stand for.

Nevertheless, the heavens and the earth are closely connected by vibratory standards, and it would pay you to familiarize yourself with the numbers of the signs in their zodiacal continuity:

ARIES, the Ram	*1*	in force in April	4
TAURUS, the Bull	*2*	in force in May	5
GEMINI, the Twins	*3*	in force in June	6
CANCER, the Crab	*4*	in force in July	7
LEO, the Lion	*5*	in force in August	8
VIRGO, the Virgin	*6*	in force in September	9
LIBRA, the Scales	*7*	in force in October	10
SCORPIO, the Scorpion	*8*	in force in November	11
SAGITTARIUS, the Archer	*9*	in force in December	12
CAPRICORN, the Goat	*10*	in force in January	1
AQUARIUS, the Water-Bearer	*11*	in force in February	2
PISCES, the Fishes	*12*	in force in March	3

We admit that there are a few—a very few—techniques used by professionals only, which also take into account the number of the sign, thus: July is the seventh calendar month, and Cancer, the Crab, in force in July, is the fourth sign of the Zodiac. The system calls for adding the *4* of Cancer to the *7* of July, with a total of *11*, a master-number. This is also the case with January, the No. 1 calendar month and Capricorn the No. 10 sign. Add *1* and *10* and again you obtain the master-number *11* for a total.

Both Cancer and Capricorn are cardinal, or leadership, signs, and certainly the *11*, as you have read repeatedly, is a tremendous vibration for mastery along vocational avenues. Look into the pages of history and you will find that the percentage of great ones born in Cancer and Capricorn is rather amazing.

But that is not the only reason why we advocate here that you familiarize yourself with the numerical values of the zodiacal signs. Adding the sign and the calendar month number reveals to you the hidden forces which function under the surface—both in a character and a human destiny.

HIDDEN NUMBERS

In concluding this book on numbers I want to emphasize that numerology does not encourage a morally dangerous fatalism. Numbers are mighty power stations in the universe and radiate energy for humans to draw from. They supply a pattern by which to guide your thoughts and your actions. Look upon numbers as an instrument upon which you can produce a harmonious tune, or you could produce discord. You are the master of your destiny, for it is all a matter of spiritual insight and moral and mental self-discipline.

All schools of metaphysical thought have made this point clear: there is an "outer" vibration or *exo*teric side and an "inner" vibration or *eso*teric angle to all forms of occult learning, and numerology is no exception. You may use the practical numerical values for your daily living and material problems. But there is also a spiritual expression to each number, called the Hidden Number. This points out the Law of Cause and Effect in human existence. "As you call into the forest, so sounds the echo."

Through meditation and a constant research into the esoteric philosophy of numbers you will soon recognize your own pattern of transmutation.

This then is the challenge of your Hidden Numbers: Dig deep for the spiritual forces within yourself, reveal them to your fellow men by good deeds and exploit their transcending stimuli when reaching for higher levels in evolution.

You cannot master the science of numbers by merely reading about it in books. You must apply this knowledge in your daily studies of

THE BOOK OF LIFE